# I TOUCH MYSELF

## LESSONS TO WAKE UP DESIRE
## & FIRE UP YOUR SEX DRIVE

### JACLYN LACEY FOSTER

Kelly,
Thank you for the
support woman.
To sparky desire ♥

Jaclyn Foster

ISBN: 978-1723044373

Book Cover design by: Lena Yang
Photo credit to: Nick Mastrolia

*To the woman who wants to be good and feel amazing...*
*in the bedroom and out.*

*You can have both.*
*The rewards are great.*
*Aliveness is inevitable.*
*You are worth it.*

# CONTENTS

Part IV
WHAT I KNOW OF PLEASURE

# DISCLAIMER
# & NOTE TO THE READER

To my close family and friends: this is your warning.

This book talks about my journey into sex and intimacy. More specifically, at times it talks about my sex life both with myself and with others.

This book breaks down the journey of how I came to be so fascinated with feeling good instead of only trying to be good and how that curiosity catapulted me into exploring sex, masturbation, and pleasure.

Although this one might be tough to swallow for those who are related to or close to me, I am committed to being a voice that celebrates sex and desire in all their consensual colors.

I have seen countless times that the more I am willing to explore sex; to talk about it, practice it, and have fun with it, the more a profound and substantial experience of pleasure runs through me in my everyday life. Not only that, but the shame I felt in exploring my sex is alchemized into the strength to be brave enough to take the actions that make me feel alive, passionate, and purpose driven. It makes me want to holler from the rooftops:

*Waking up your desire is okay!*
*It's okay to ask for what you want,*
*and to have it.*

This book is definitely not for you if you don't want the visual in your head of me naked and/or it makes you uncomfortable to think about having a conversation with me about sex-related topics. Please know that it gets raw and unfiltered at times.

It was my intention to be as real and true to my experience and voice as possible, even when it wasn't pretty or "appropriate," because, well, that's life. It was important to me that this book be as unfiltered as I could muster so that others could connect deeper with its relevance to their own inner process and, possibly, unspoken desires.

I would also recommend putting this book down before the Five Stages of Desire section, if you find the topic of non-monogamy unthinkable.

Finally, I would also say this book is not for you if you know my boyfriend and I personally and think that your feelings towards us could be affected if you didn't share the same relationship and intimacy choices as us. If you are in our lives and you love us, we want it to stay that way, and we will respect our differences. We have found our choices to be rewarding and wouldn't change a thing, but we also know that not everyone agrees with or chooses the same path.

With that said, this book is for you if you are intrigued by the concept of living a life you desire and by doing what it takes to prioritize feeling good both in and out of the bedroom. It's for you if you are curious about how to align more with your desires, how to embrace yourself as a sexual being, and how to navigate the wide world of sexual desire.

It is for you if you are sexually curious and trying to figure yourself or your partner out. It is also for you if you feel like there is a sexual part of yourself that has been dormant that could use some awakening.

For those who continue to read, although I have changed many names and some minor details in this book to protect the privacy of those that are weaved into this story, the words I write about myself are all true accounts of my experiences.

So, for those of you who are still with me, let's do this! It's been a long time coming.

# INTRODUCTION

The year of my twenty-ninth birthday I was faced with a life question that I just couldn't shake: Why can't I touch myself?

It was time to know. I was kinda desperate. No, who am I kidding? I was extremely desperate and downright pleasure-hungry. Super sexy combination, right?

Not only was I pleasure-hungry, I was also pleasure-resistant. Talk about a situation of having one foot on the gas, the other on the brakes, and being nothing but stuck in the mud.

It felt crazy to me to think I had reached twenty-nine years on this planet without masturbating. I was so out of touch with my body that the thought of touching it actually repulsed me. I was clueless as to what it meant to have an orgasm, and I didn't touch myself intimately unless I was washing myself in the shower, wiping myself in the bathroom, or accidentally brushing myself as I passed by a piece of furniture.

I was about forty pounds overweight and struggling heavily with showing any skin even in the hottest heat of the summer. On top of that, I felt like I was always talking about how tired, overwhelmed, and burned out I was. Seriously, all the time.

I don't know what bothered me more: being a sad, sad story of the misfit woman who was void of sexual pleasure and feelings of desire for her life and herself, or that I felt so run down so often that I was disengaging from the world in a way that felt rotten.

Feeling disconnected with my body, my sex, and my pleasure felt wrong on a cellular level. The desire for sexual exploration and making the topic part of my conversations in life became firmly planted within me.

I was hungry (more like starving) in both the sex and the aliveness departments of life, and it was not a good look. As my hunger grew, I was driven to dive into exploring desire, pleasure, sex, orgasm, and intimacy. All those words were like a sweet-sounding foreign language I desperately wanted to learn.

There was something inside of me that was convinced my journey of exploring desire and sex would translate into more aliveness.

I can tell you, as I learned the language of these words and what they meant for me, there was so much juicy goodness to discover. It makes me so thrilled to be able to spread the word, and my legs.

Sex, in my eyes, seems to have been placed into the category of things we all know that we do but don't really talk about because we've been taught that it isn't socially

acceptable. You know, like death, pooping, or worse...
women farting (gasp!).

We make references, and we may joke, but how often do
we honestly have real conversations about sexual desire
with our partners and those that can help us get more out
of what we want? We beat around the bush instead of
getting right in there.

I understand that things can get tangled up and hairy in
there, but let's switch that up, shall we? It might get dark
and messy at times, *and* it's worth it.

I can tell you with certainty that what I have learned has
improved my sex life with myself and others (I can now
masturbate and enjoy it, massive hell yes!), has led me to
finally being orgasmic (with myself and others), and, most
importantly, has led to me feeling good and alive with
enthusiasm for my present and future.

## FEEL BETTER BY FEELING GOOD

This book has been broken down into four sections. At
the end of each chapter, there will be an opportunity for
you to do an exercise (a "spark") to stimulate your
version of exploring the topic. I call these exercises
"sparks" because I like to visualize my internal feel-good
meter as a fire. Every time I follow what I want and
need, I stoke the internal fire and allow it to grow. With
each spark you read and respond to, you will have the
opportunity to strengthen your own internal flame of
desire.

In the first section, Questioning the Rules, I share how I
started to question the rules around sex and pleasure and

the golden rule I use when it comes to deciding whether or not it's worth going down a particular road of desire.

In the second section, I break down eleven lessons I've learned on my path to waking up desire and how you can apply these lessons to your life as well.

In the third section, I share the five stages of desire I keep in mind when living out a desire. They are beneficial, especially with bigger desires, to help give me structure and steps when I notice I am feeling stuck or scared. I share a very intimate desire of mine in this section and how listening to and following this desire has changed my life forever.

I close the book with sharing what I know of pleasure and the nuggets that I have taken forward with me in my everyday life to help me stay on track when I find myself running out of steam and forgetting my connection to desire.

I am super confident that these steps can help you too. Even if you only choose to take one or two of these lessons and practice them regularly, you will notice shifts in the way you see yourself and your relationship with desire and sex.

As I type these words, I feel giggly and excited inside knowing that you are about to tap into these truths for yourself. You are so worth it. There is no time like the present to give yourself the gift of listening to your desire and giving in to the pull of your body, begging you to surrender to your sexual self.

Your future self will thank you.

# PART I
# QUESTIONING THE RULES

# BEING A GOOD GIRL

I grew up with rules. I was told by my parents, teachers, media, government, and religion what I needed to do to be considered a good girl in society. I bet, if you are a woman, you can relate. If you are a man, you probably heard what you need to do to be considered a *Man*. Different roles, different rules. As I think a lot of us do, I did my best to obey those rules to keep a good reputation.

I worked extra hard to steer clear of what was "bad." Sex, alcohol, or drugs; if it had a stigma, I had nothing to do with it. When it came time to determine the most righteous choice, WWJD (What Would Jaclyn Do) was the question my friends would ask.

I think that those who knew me in my childhood and teenage years will be surprised to see this book coming from me and will laugh out loud remembering that I was voted most likely to be a nun out of my friends in our high school class. It didn't make the yearbook, but it was the ongoing joke.

I didn't touch things that weren't mine. I didn't touch myself (what respectable person does?). I tried to be nice and keep the peace so that others would be happy. I didn't try to dress too pretty or sexy because that just draws attention. I didn't want to run the risk of being seen as slutty or inappropriate, and, besides, I didn't have the body for it anyway. I was a gymnast as a child and had more of a muscular build. I wasn't really feminine enough to dress sexy anyway, so why try?

A focus on feeling good was nowhere to be found. I have a faint memory of a moment on the playground with one of those steel swinging bars between my legs pushed up against *my private parts*. (Hey, I didn't know what to call "them" as a kid.) I squeezed my legs together to increase the pressure, and I felt a pulsing between my legs. It felt good. It increased as my classmates ran back into the school after recess, and I lingered in the sensation of it a bit longer because I had no idea what I was discovering.

I swung myself down, lowering to the ground, and *poof* it was gone as quickly as it came. I don't know what was going on in my little brain, but I certainly didn't associate that feeling with sex.

Me, sexual?!

Never.

And yeah, you could say, "You were just a kid, of course you weren't going to associate yourself with being sexual!" And that may be true, but even into my teenage years I was not on the same page as my sexually curious friends.

I had a strong association that sex occurred between a man and woman who made a choice to be together monogamously for the rest of their lives and only once they are married, of course. It was actually more than just being married that was required. I remember hearing that only parents have sex. Now I chuckle as I think back to when I thought I had to have a child to have sex.

My parents met as teenagers, were high school sweethearts and married in their twenties. That can be a tough act to follow in today's day in age. It took me some time to be okay with the fact that it doesn't make me a "bad" girl to choose my own relationship and sexual path.

In addition to seeing long-term monogamy as *the* option, sex also meant babies, and I had no desire to be a young mommy. I did not want that responsibility for myself or my parents. The fear of babies alone was enough to scare me away from the boys.

Over the years, I felt like my classmates were experimenting with each other and themselves, but I was very much cut off from it all. I remember a few of my girlfriends telling me that they had tried kissing another girl and other friends sharing their first times having sex or messing around with other boys.

I really couldn't fathom this. As a result of my detachment, I did not think of myself as sexual or sexually appealing in any way. Don't get me wrong, some boys thought I was cute and liked me. I was just terrified of them.

I remember getting a letter mailed to my home address in elementary school by a classmate asking me if I would be his girlfriend. In his note, he gave instructions to circle YES or NO and mail the letter back to him. I remember smiling and enjoying it while simultaneously being paralyzed with the fear of what either answer implied.

There were other private moments where I felt sensation in my private parts as a child which bordered on feeling good, but there was so much guilt associated with the feeling that I never explored it further.

One night I lay awake feeling like my genitals were on fire and like I needed to itch or touch them. I don't remember anything being wrong with me, or any need for medical attention, there was just a lot of sensation, and I didn't know what to do with it.

I remember telling someone I saw as an authority figure in my life about it and being told not to touch "it" (meaning my itchy private parts), and in my little brain, I made an association that touching my private parts was not a good idea. All these voices, influences, and rules triggered a series of associations that shut down my relationship with my body and my sexuality.

*Don't touch yourself* became an internal mantra of mine, along with *don't have sex before you're married*, and *don't talk about sex at all.*

Be good.

# BREAKING THE RULES

My journey towards sexual liberation did not start with venturing out in my sex with others or even with myself. It began with questioning some of the rules around what it meant to be good.

It took me until about my college years when I was out of my parents' house to start questioning the rules. This is not a knock at my parents. It's just a truth. Living outside the comfort and safety of my parents' house forced me to think for myself in a way I hadn't ever done before.

Being in college became a place where I started to question some of those rules you read about earlier. It was easy for me to get sucked into the fantasy: these four years are where I figure out the rest of my life. I thought many times as I started my freshman year, "This is when I will define my long-term career path, find my life partner, and clearly establish my life trajectory." Of course, at thirty-five writing this book, I chuckle, that is not the way it went down.

At this time, my college mind was pretty fixed on my relationship/sex plan. I would get married (never divorced), my man would meet my sexual needs (I would not), and we would be monogamous for life.

It took me until my sophomore year for this plan to be shaken. I was hitting a high in my life. I was on the cross-country team and running faster than I ever had. I was feeling better in my skin and was the thinnest I had ever been. I felt better putting clothes on and was playing with dressing in ways that felt prettier and sexier. I was getting more attention from guys, and I was curious about it.

One of those guys was named Ben, one of my classmates that became a study partner. Study partners turned into going out on a date, and that turned into boyfriend and girlfriend, and I was in love. Looking back now, I'm not even sure what the glue was that stuck us together for as long as we were. The relationship lasted about a year.

He was one of my first boyfriends and my first sexual partner. I flew out to see him during one of my school breaks. It felt like a fairytale finding a dress to wear that he would see me in as he picked me up at the airport. Oh, the fantasy of an airport reunion.

Being that he was my first what I would consider semi-adult relationship, and my first sexual experience, I was heartbroken when I learned that this would not be my last relationship.

Towards the end of our relationship, I found out through the grapevine that Ben had been cheating on me, and there were a number of people who knew about it. Not one of them said anything to me. There were signs. He didn't want to have sex anymore.

I remember him saying something along the lines of, "I don't feel right about having sex out of wedlock anymore." *Huh? Come again.* I felt grateful he had a conscience and didn't have sex with both of us at the same time but, *really dude?* It felt so fake hearing these words fumble out of his lips.

Around this time, I had a conversation with my mom about how unhappy I was and how much I wished he would just break up with me. My mom said to me, "Jaclyn, do you realize that you could just break up with him?" Honestly, until that moment, I didn't.

Shortly after that conversation, I found out the truth through one of Ben's friends. He took me outside at a party and told me that he thought I should know. Ben had been hooking up with someone else for the last few months.

I knew the relationship was over. I ended it, finally! It broke my heart to do it. I always thought if I were cheated on, I would run far away and never look back. I have found that is easier said than done. I used to think that relationship decisions could be black and white. I thought I would effortlessly be able to switch off my emotions and leave someone without turning back if they cheated on me. I know now that in intimate relationships where love, emotions and shared experiences are involved, staying *and* leaving can get *very* grey.

On top of the cheating, I was also pissed that others around me knew this was happening and no one said anything. I felt like these so-called friends I had weren't what I thought they were.

For months, I turned to binging on chocolate chip granola, ice cream, and gummy candies by the bag as my weight shot up. I blamed the dryers for shrinking my clothes. I was in a bit of denial.

While we were together, I poured so much energy into Ben and this concept of *us* that I lost just about every ounce of myself. It was a hard lesson for me to learn that no matter how much I love someone and want to make them happy, the more I do for them and grasp to save the relationship, the more I end up smothering it. The result: the relationship dies, I'm exhausted, and I lose myself.

This relationship was the end of the fairytale hope and the start of figuring out a way to be in relationships in a way that was more sustainable. My naïve and blind faith that commitment was a given when a relationship starts turned into more of curiosity over the years: How does a relationship actually stay strong and last long? Is it possible? Is it worth it?

It also meant the whole "monogamous for life" idea I had stuck in my head was blown out of the water. I broke that rule. A seed was planted for some new possibilities: Is sex for more than love and baby making? And why do I feel so guilty about exploring the thought of it?

This relationship was a catalyst to questioning my relationship to my intimate partners and my sexual self. My light for life was out, and I didn't know where to find it. It was time to experiment with a different way of relating.

We'll get more in-depth as to how I found my light again in the eleven lessons, but since we are talking about rules, I'd like to share one I commit myself to as a woman who listens to her desire. It's a rule I've made for myself because it feels good to follow it. What a concept, right? Doing something because it feels good. Let's talk more about that.

# THE GOLDEN RULE

I want to offer up my Golden Rule. This rule is something I have come to know from this journey of exploring pleasure and how I started to adapt and change my old rules in a way that would work for who I wanted to become.

The rule is this: *If it makes me feel good, I want to do it, and if it doesn't hurt or sabotage myself or another person, I'm going to **do it**. I'll try it once, or perhaps a few times, and see how I feel from there.*

It may seem impractical, time-consuming or not make sense to my busy mind, but I have learned the value of following desire. When I'm smart and paying attention, I listen and let it lead me.

## A MEMORY

A couple of years ago I had the opportunity of getting to know an incredibly loving and welcoming woman who passed away when she was far too young from lung cancer. Her name was Gerri. She was my boyfriend's mother, and I had the pleasure of knowing her intimately in the last year of her life. This friendship offered me many beautiful gifts. One was a deep connection to my mortality with the reminder of how fleeting life can be, and another was the experience of how truly vital the simplest, smallest actions can be in bringing joy.

Towards the end, we would sit together and I would listen to stories of where she lived during her lifetime, what she did and didn't do, and how she might do some things differently could she do it again.

Gerri called me the Energizer Bunny (shortened to Bunny) because I was always doing *something*. There was a funny moment when a hospice doctor came to the house and heard everyone calling me Bunny, so the doctor called me Bunny feeling confident that it was my birth-given first name. All present, including Gerri, my boyfriend and some close relatives, started to laugh as we realized how much the nickname had stuck.

We even learned that in her Amazon purchase cart right before she passed was a larger-than-life-sized Energizer Bunny stuffed animal which she had planned to buy for me. Her boys took pleasure in completing that order and giving me the bunny after her passing. Every time I look at it, it makes me smile to remember her and the valuable lessons she taught me.

I would often find myself going over to the house to help out with cleaning out cupboards, doing chores, and asking what I could do to make things a bit easier. One day when I finished the dishes, I came in and asked her what I could do next. She looked at me and made a request: "You've been doing a lot around here, and I appreciate it, but I'd love if you'd sit down and talk to me. You don't need to do so much all the time."

It stopped me in my tracks to realize that it's not always about *doing* the next thing. There is more to life than checking off my to-do list.

Once she passed, as we sat at the heartwarming funeral service for Gerri, the woman facilitating shared a poem by Mary Oliver that starts off with the words, "You do not have to be good." As I heard those words, tears started to stream down my face.

I cried as I thought about Gerri's life, my life, and the lives of so many I know who struggle to let these words sink in.

*You do not have to be good.*

I realized the golden rule that day in a more profound way than I ever had.

The facilitator of the ceremony continued to read the words of Mary Oliver's poem, *Wild Geese*:

> *You do not have to walk on your knees*
> *For a hundred miles through the desert, repenting.*
> *You only have to let the soft animal of your body*
> *love what it loves.*

Wait.

It doesn't all have to be about struggle?

I can let my body love what it loves?

I was profoundly moved, and I felt a compulsion to

remember to ask myself moving forward: Does it make me feel good?

WHAT I MEAN...

When I talk about feeling good, I'm talking about the nourishing things that fill me up and make me want to do and be more. I mean those things that fill me with a sense of completion, gratitude, and aliveness. What I want more of are the desires that start to take over my being in a beautiful way, filling me with conviction and trust in who I am. That's the good stuff.

This is what a fulfilling life is made of in my opinion: expanding my life focus to more and more of what makes me feel good so that I can radiate that joy out into the world.

WHAT I DON'T MEAN...

There are things we do that feel good but are forms of self-sabotage. These are the things we do to overcompensate for something or to "reward" ourselves in a way that feels bad shortly after we have done it.

Examples of this are: getting drunk after a tough day instead of resetting with a healthy self-care routine, eating a box of cookies after a frustrating encounter when we know we want to lose weight, or binge-watching an entire series of reruns over the weekend because you are tired instead of asking yourself what you really need to recharge. We've all been there.

What I've learned is that these things don't *really* feel

good anyway; they feel familiar. Familiar can sometimes be disguised as feeling good because it is safe and known, but it often tends to feel stale, old, and unappetizing when we realize it's time for something new.

These short-term, misleading feel-goods are not the goal here. The goal is to feel genuinely good in a sustainable way. As we start the lessons, I will share the critical question I now ask as a guide to figure out what makes me feel good.

But first, here's your spark to kindle your own internal flame.

*Split up a piece of paper into two columns. On one column write, "be good" and on the other, "feel good."*

*Under the "be good" column, write down all the ways you do good. By do good, I mean all the things you feel you "should" do because someone is asking it of you or because you are under the impression that it is an obligation under the role you play as a woman, a mother, a girlfriend, an employee, etc.*

*Perhaps you also think of it as what you do to follow the rules, what is expected of you by others, or meets the requirements of what a respectable person in your position would do. You can enjoy it or not. The point is to get honest with yourself about what you do for the sake of "being good."*

*Under the "feel good" column, write down the things you do just because you want to. Write down the things you do because you like how they feel and how they give energy, the things you do just for you. Whether or not you do it to be good is irrelevant, all that matters is that you want to do it.*

*Once you have completed both columns, take a look at each. Is one longer than the other? Do the columns overlap at all? Do you realize in looking at these columns that you spend more time in the "do good" department?*

*To ignite this spark, choose one thing on the "feel good" list that gets you excited. When was the last time you did it?*

*Can you set aside some time for it in the next twenty-four hours?*

# PART II
# ELEVEN LESSONS
# TO WAKE UP DESIRE

# THE MOST IMPORTANT QUESTION

"What do you want to do today?" my mom asked me. I sat with a blank face and looked back at her. "I don't know." It was a regular day. There was nothing special about it except for the realization that I didn't know how to answer the question. What do *I* want? I was stumped. But, oh, I had friends that could help me out with that one, and they did.

I forfeited my right to choose what I wanted and let my friends take over as the decision-makers for that day. I remember feeling like I wanted others to be happy around me, so I let them choose. I didn't even think about putting my desires first. As you might be guessing, although this specific day stuck out in my mind, putting the desires of others above my own was the usual for me.

This day of unlimited options proposed to me as a child in grade school turned into an excursion to a water park and a "stay-up." A stay-up was something our parents invented where we would watch TGIF together and hang out until 10 pm at one of the neighborhood friends' houses.

I enjoyed the day, I guess...

But was it really what I wanted to do?

It wasn't my idea.

The question I have learned that is unavoidable for a life of feeling good is: What do I want?

I'm learning to ask myself this question again and again until one day, I hope, it becomes as natural as brushing my teeth in the morning.

I was at a women's workshop one day a few years ago, and the woman leading the talk asked us to raise our hands if we would be willing to make one sexual request of our partners. I was in shock at the fact that I saw less than one-third of the women raise their hands.

There were over a hundred of us in the room. What's going on with us women that we don't either feel comfortable enough to ask for something we want or flat out don't know what we would even say?

Although a part of me was shocked, I remembered that as a child when I was asked what I wanted to do, I had no answer. I don't know about you, but as a woman, a sister, and a wife, I often took the role of helper, nurturer, and caretaker starting from a very young age. Those roles required me to observe what needed to be done for things to go smoothly and to take care of whatever it was with a smile.

Thinking about my desires and needs was a much-delayed afterthought if it even came up at all. I know from seeing other women in my life that, at the very least, this is not unusual. Nurturing and giving seems like the thing to do to be a "good" woman. Receiving and letting ourselves be nurtured, not so much. It has been a slow and steady process for me, but thinking and acting on what I want has played a critical role in living a more fulfilling life.

The simple and honest truth is that if we don't ask, we don't know. Knowing what we want can take time to cultivate. I think we hesitate to ask what we want for a few reasons.

One, we want others around us to be happy, and we don't want to rock the boat. I have to be careful with this one, as I fall into this category. I can become a giggly approval-seeking school girl that wants others to like me and will do whatever they want to make sure they are happy.

This reason seemed innocent and generous enough, until BAM. One day I woke up and realized all I did was make others happy. Let me tell you, when I finally woke up to this I was irritated. Nagging thoughts arose, "How long can you keep this up? This isn't sustainable." I also heard myself say, "I can't handle one more person asking me to do something. I'm done."

Here's the paradox: when I try exclusively to make others happy, I end up less happy and the relationship becomes more based on dependence and an attempt to seek approval. When I strive to make myself happy, others have the space to make themselves happy, and we can bring our good feelings back to each other in order to flourish together.

I've noticed that by living in a way where I am striving to make myself happy first, there is a chance for interdependence in our relationship. We love each other and do for each other without losing ourselves in the process. For me, this is not the easiest thing to do, but it is extremely rewarding.

Two, it requires experimentation to figure out what we want. I did not know my body well enough to tell anyone what I wanted for a very long time (like until I was 30). I would get frustrated with sex because I wasn't having orgasms, but I hadn't even touched myself to learn what felt good in my body. How was I going to be able to tell someone else how I liked it?

And three, asking for what we want can feel awkward. What if someone thinks we are weird or strange because of our desires? What if they say no? What if that person no longer wants to be in our life as a result?

Stepping into your desire can be scary. Here's the thing though...

## IT MATTERS

What you want matters.

I will repeat. What you want matters.

Say it with me now: What I want matters!

(I can't hear you. Say it out loud...right now, just for fun!)

Those that love you, like *truly* love you and respect you and the interactions you have with them, will be cool with answering your questions and creating dialogue when you ask for something.

When I first had desires come up to ask my boyfriend David to go slower or to finger me more often while he went down on me, I waited for months of wanting him to do it more before I asked. Initially, when I wanted it, I kind of just waited a while on blind hope, not opening my mouth to actually put in a request. I tried to be a Jedi master, willing him to slip a finger in there every time I wanted him to.

The man is supposed to be reading my mind, goddammit. Give me some of that blind hope miracle action. Did he not get the memo that in long-term relationships we start to learn mind-reading abilities magically?

It was like standing in line at the hotdog stand, being up at the counter and not opening my mouth to place my order. How are they going to know what I want if I don't ask for it?

What was the worst that could happen? He could say no, or he could say *yes*. Didn't I want to know if I had a man who was willing to say yes? You would think so, but alas, for a while I felt as though I didn't want to rock the boat and find out. It felt good enough.

I have found that looking at the way I ask my partner for what I want gives excellent insight into what I ask for in general in my life and to the universe. Knowing I tend to give more than feels good, I try to tune into how I ask for what I want from my partner.

When I fall into old habits, I'll ask what he wants and forget, ignore, and maybe even minimize (*ugh, that's the worst!*) my own needs and desires. When I realize I'm doing it, I'll check in to see in what other areas of my life I'm sacrificing my desires for some reason or some*one*; and, often, I won't have to look hard to find them. I'll be unnecessarily overworking myself or trying to take care of more chores at home than feels good for the sake of "getting it done."

I'm now very weary of my thought process when I hastily say to myself, "Ugh, I'm just going to get it done." That usually means for me, "You're going to have resentment, woman. Think twice." The thing is, often no one is asking me to overwork myself; I put it on myself. It's a habit I'm trying to break, but one that I fear many women share: to put every want and need around them above their own, finding any number of reasons to justify why they can't choose their desire.

Start asking: What do I want? Ask, ask, and ask some more. One of the most significant recommendations I can give if you are new to desire is to ask yourself this question daily. Without this question, your relationship with desire will not begin.

# SPARK

*In the privacy of your own home in a space that feels safe and comfortable, pull out a favorite pen and notebook and set a timer for five minutes. Close your eyes and ask yourself, "What do I want?"*

*Take a few deep breaths and notice your feet on the floor and the weight of your buttocks in your chair, and then open your eyes and start writing, "I want..." and finish the sentence. When you finish that sentence, start another one with "I want..." and keep going.*

*There are no wrong answers. You are starting your relationship with desire. Yippie!*

# YOU'VE GOT TO FIND IT FROM WITHIN

The question "What do I want?" is closely linked to your ability to connect with the priceless gift you have of giving yourself permission. Let me tell you how I started a relationship with my desire by giving myself permission to fly halfway around the world.

I was twenty-two years old when I boarded the plane that would take me to Auckland, New Zealand. I remember sitting at LAX on my layover wondering what the hell I was doing, and what had made me think I was strong enough to take this trip.

I had been out of the country for a study abroad program in Sweden a few years earlier, but this was different. There would be a lot less structure and support. I was going alone and didn't have a soul waiting for me on the other side.

Why was I going to New Zealand?

For one, a friend told me the sushi was delicious there, and honestly, up until this moment in my life, I felt like I hadn't made many decisions that came from my desire. I felt an urge to leave the country to do some soul-searching.

This trip was a declaration of my independence. A choice made by me, for me. Something that was extremely new and exhilarating. Um, yeah, I was scared shitless at the airport. I couldn't stomach my food from the airport terminal food court and was flooded with confusion and doubt as nausea, lightheadedness, and paralysis kicked in.

Was this feeling a sign that I was about to plunge headfirst into the worst decision of my life? Or was it nothing more than nervous butterflies which meant I was stepping outside of my comfort zone?

What was it that drove me to think this could be good for me? Was this a desperate move that would land me deeper in the hole of life confusion? Or could this be a game changer that would provide me with greater clarity as to my life direction?

I was so exhausted when I stepped onto the plane that I fell dead asleep for eight hours straight as soon as I sat down. I looked over at the woman in the seat next to me as my eyes started to open, and she jokingly shared that she was glad to see me alive after being out for so long. We arrived at the Auckland airport safely, and I made my way to my hostel at 5:00 am shortly before the sunrise.

As I made my way to the hostel, I reflected on the conversation I had with a woman walking down the airport terminal who was returning home to New Zealand after ten years away. This was her homecoming. I couldn't help but think that this trip in some ways was also a homecoming for me. A long physical trip to find a way back to myself. *One could only hope!*

The first two weeks were by far the hardest. I had left my boyfriend, family and friends behind. I couldn't even contact my family on the same day because we were in such different time zones, which felt *far*! This was before the age of Skype, I had to use a calling card with a time limit from the international exchange office in order to connect with friends and family.

I would be living out of a backpack for the next six months of my visa and felt strongly that no matter how lonely and strange these first days felt, I was going to follow through. Part of what kept me in New Zealand was knowing that even though I loved those I had left behind, I wasn't meant to be back in my home town right now. I knew if I flew back, I'd probably feel even more lost.

GETTING THERE

After acclimating in Auckland for a couple weeks, I boarded a bus to a little coastal town southeast of the city. It was the cutest little town with one main street where you could find many small shops, including the one I would be working at. The town was painted with a massive hill of homes from top to bottom with an incredible ocean view and beautiful Pohutukawa trees that ran along the coast with their colorful red flowers.

As the bus pulled up to my new home for the next couple months, I looked for the man who I had arranged to pick me up. I would be working for him at the shop he owned, which was multifunctional; a jewelry accessory shop with a laundromat and a computer repair spot, all in one. Only in New Zealand have I ever seen such a gloriously versatile shop where so many things could be done all at once. I would work at the register and live right above the shop for a couple of months.

I found the job a couple months before I boarded the plane. The shop owner and I had coordinated through email weeks prior arranging for him to pick me up at the bus station. He would later tell me that, of all the people he had come and stay with him to work for his shop, I was the one with the most questions. Hey, I like to know what I'm getting into! Let's just say spontaneity hasn't always been my strong suit.

As I got into his car, the thought crossed my mind that I could very well die here in the next few minutes. I asked myself how I could trust someone with my life that I had only communicated with a few times via email. I had no lifeline to reach out to in case of emergency, and I had no idea about how 9-1-1 worked out there. Was 9-1-1 a universal thing?

We arrived at our location fast. Faster than I wanted to because I was afraid of what might happen once I settled in and realized what I had done. You know, fly across the world and decide to live and work in a place where I was a complete stranger. This trip was not feeling like a vacation anymore.

We had been driving for less than ten minutes when we pulled up to an alley-like entrance and parked the car facing a shed-like entrance with rusted metal doors. I was sure of it...yup, I had come here to die. He was going to shove me through the door, and my death would be waiting for me on the other side—perhaps by knife, poison, or some other torture method.

What did I come here for again? What was about to happen? He seemed kind enough; he had a smile on his face, but I was so overloaded with newness and stimulation that I felt like I was about to combust. Mind-blown felt like an understatement at this moment.

## SMALL TOWN, BIG LESSON

Much to my relief, I did not die. I settled into my job and temporary life. The shed door entrance opened up to an oversized garage space with a bunch of tools, a small gym-like area, and a stairway which led up to a small three-bed apartment. Below the apartment was where I would sit at the cash register for the next few months with Norah Jones' *Come Away With Me* album as my soundtrack.

One day, a friend of the owner's walked in. I remember him walking in with a big smile, radiating a particular kind of zest for life that looked delicious. His name was Matt, and he was looking for temporary workers to help with his business ventures. He looked like he was enjoying life and doing something right. I had extra time, and I wanted what he was having.

Goodness, I was desperate to be living differently. Did I tell you yet that I felt uncomfortably overweight? I had a poor relationship with my body. It didn't matter how hot it was outside; I would still wear multiple layers. It was a daily habit to be casually dressed with a sports bra, sweatshirt, and stretchy pants on.

Shit, honestly, I didn't even care how I looked. Well, I did and I didn't. I was ashamed of my body, so it was easier to cover up and pretend I didn't care. Life was already taking up too much energy, caring about the way I looked was just too much. If it was a day I had to go out and interact with the world, I wanted that sweatshirt covering me up so it was one less thing to worry about and deal with.

I didn't have a career direction or purpose. I knew that what I had done so far in my life was not exciting me, and I was with a boyfriend that I knew deep down I didn't want to be with.

Tom, my boyfriend at the time, was someone I knew from my teenage years that happened to pop back into my life after college at a time where I felt like I was wandering aimlessly through the world searching for something stable to latch on to. We were from the same town. He was familiar, and I knew there were times off and on when he wanted something with me in the past. It felt nice to know I was wanted. We reacquainted and found ourselves in a relationship.

When I left for New Zealand, we planned to stay together and try a long-distance relationship. The thing was, the longer I was in New Zealand, the more I felt that we probably should have called it quits before I got on the plane.

This trip was not at all about hooking up or looking for a man in any capacity, but it also wasn't meant to be for holding back. I was in limbo. Email him to end the relationship? Or keep it going just in case I decide at the end of this I still want to be with him in some capacity? I didn't feel confident about either choice, so I didn't make one.

Even though I had no idea what to do about Tom, I can say that when Matt walked into the shop full of life, with 100% certainty, I was thinking, *"Yes, please."* He was a man who was going after his passion with an open heart, bringing play, coupled with drive and determination, to his venture. I ended up working for him for a couple of months in addition to my job at the shop. He taught me how to drive a stick shift around the small town. We went on runs, and I would help him clean and take care of tasks for his business.

I will never forget one day when we were talking about life. I was probably processing through not knowing what I was going to do at the end of the six months, thinking about the fact that I had a business economics degree, had worked in a corporate environment for a miserable year, and felt completely unsure about what would make me feel better about my life when I got back to the States.

Matt looked at me and gave me the most valuable lesson I learned from my New Zealand trip, one that has replayed in my head and heart countless times since that day.

He said to me, "Jaclyn, you are the only person you have to live with 24/7."

He reminded me that with every decision I make, I am the only one that has to live with it day in and day out. I am the one that has to live with the consequences of taking and not taking action for myself.

He taught me that it doesn't matter who is in my life and to what capacity. I will always be the only one I spend every second of every day with, so it might be worth making sure that I feel right about the actions I am taking and that I am doing them because I want to.

In his firm yet lighthearted and playful manner, Matt reinforced that not only does what I want matter, but that ultimately I'm the only one that can decide whether or not I'm going to give myself permission to have it.

I don't remember anyone up until that point in my life who so wholeheartedly encouraged me to put myself first.

## THE IMPOSSIBLE

It's incredible what can happen when there is chemistry and gratitude in a connection and how much of an impact it can make. I felt so much value from my relationship with Matt that I started to think about what it would be like to be with him.

For the first couple months of knowing him, I thought it impossible that Matt could want anything with me besides my help on his business projects and perhaps a buddy. Matt was older than me by about eight years, or maybe it was more than that. Between the age difference and the business-like relationship we had, I thought he'd never see me as an option romantically.

There is no way he thought about me sexually. I didn't end things with Tom. Why would I? I was feeling everything out. Nothing was going to happen anyway.

As the weeks passed though, I wasn't so sure anymore. We started to spend a bit more time with each other outside of work. We'd make lunch together and play games out in the backyard. We always seemed to play, laugh, and enjoy each other's company. Was this just our way of making our responsibilities fun? Or could he be interested in me romantically? I was starting to fantasize about the latter.

Well, one day Matt and I were sitting on the couch watching Napoleon Dynamite as friends, and before I knew it, we were lying on the couch...cuddled up together, spooning. *Wait!* How did it happen? I had no idea, but I wasn't about to stop it.

I remember when he made his move to put his arm around me, I was thinking, "This can't be real, what is happening?" But *it was happening.* My pussy woke up and was in a state of bliss as we kissed. We made out for a while, and I spent the night. We did not have sex. I was starting to create new rules and adapt the old, but having sex the first time I made out with someone was not an option. Even if he was the most amazing person I could imagine being with.

I woke up the next day and had a moment of guilt as it hit me, "*Shit,* I kind of just cheated on Tom." Even though I felt more and more like we were moving towards a breakup, I hadn't ended it yet. I gave myself leeway as we were on different sides of the globe. I was doing my best.

How could I know that Matt was going to make a move? I emailed Tom that day saying that it would be best if we ended our commitment until I got back. It wasn't the end of my communication with him on that trip, but it was the end of our relationship.

Any hope of continuation when I returned dissolved

through our miscommunications over the rest of my trip. Tom was hurt at the thought of me meeting someone new, and I felt he wasn't being honest with me about being faithful back at home. Everything between us felt shady and full of half-truths.

Throughout the rest of my six months in New Zealand, even though I went in and out of living in and visiting this small town, Matt and I stayed in touch and had a few intimate connections. Curiously enough, the day I finally had sex with him was also the day I got on the plane to head back to the States. The girl that at one time thought she would only have sex with one person in her whole life, was now having sex with a person she may never see again and then running off to the airport.

It made it harder to go, and I beat myself up a bit for doing it because of that reason, but I did *not* want to let go. At the moment, the opportunity for intimacy and his touch was something I clung to because I knew it was so fleeting.

When I returned to Boston after my New Zealand adventure, I felt as though I was in love with Matt, in an intense and longing way that my heart might never heal from. When I got off the plane, my parents had to convince me to get in the car to go home. I wanted to buy a ticket right then and head back to New Zealand.

Yes, you read that right. I didn't even want to leave the airport to get dinner. I wanted to get right back on another flight that would bring me back to Auckland. On that flight home, I could not stop crying. The flood gates opened and I could not stop them. We are talking a twelve-hour flight and a *long* layover of continuous weeping with red eyes and snotty boogies and, oh, yes... there was sobbing involved. It was not pretty, not at all.

As time passed, I realized the loss and sadness I felt stemmed from the gratitude for the lesson of self-permission and approval along with the fear that I might not be able to give myself that gift in the same way he had. He embodied unapologetic permission in my eyes.

I wanted to hold on tight and not let go, keeping him as my symbol for the permission I wished I could give myself. It felt a lot more comfortable to receive permission from someone outside of myself that I saw as strong and capable as opposed to trying to dig deep within and risk not finding it. Finding it within myself meant that I had to drop the constant approval seeking and trust myself to be a strong and capable woman. Just as I am.

I look back now and see that without self-permission, there would be no desire or pleasure. I had to learn to own it. It's vital to surround ourselves with others that encourage us to believe and trust in ourselves, but ultimately, we have to give ourselves the final go ahead.

PERMISSION NOW

If I could have a fairy godmother drop any special pixie dust over me, it would be permission dust. I'd have a big old dumpster-sized container of it dropped off and plopped into the backyard so that I could do a daily dive into it. I'd get right up in there and stuff my face in it and roll around in it like I was a puppy rolling around blissfully on freshly cut grass.

I love infusing my day with a sprinkle of permission dust.

There are so many fun ways to play with this. As you pour your sugar on your morning coffee, let that be your permission powder for the day. As you brush your teeth, spray your perfume, or spread your lip gloss on your lips, imagine it to be full of permission dust to give you the strength to choose for yourself that day.

Let's fast-forward twelve years from my time in New Zealand for a moment, to when I signed up for a course I had been wanting to enroll in for years. For some reason I felt the need to ask my current boyfriend David for permission. We don't share finances, and we don't have any agreed-upon obligation or commitment that we tell each other about our purchases, but I felt I needed to ask him if he was okay with it.

When I received his full support, it came down to whether or not I was able to say yes to myself. It felt a bit scary to connect again with the fact that I would be the only one holding myself back if I said no. A part of me had wanted him to push back more because I was nervous about saying yes to myself.

The truth of knowing that I am the only one who matters in the desire department is equally confronting and liberating. It's a "yeah baby" and "oh shit" sandwich, which sometimes goes down smoothly and other times makes me wonder if I'll be able to stomach it.

# SPARK

*What you want matters. You get to decide if you are up for giving yourself permission to have it. Choose environments and surround yourself with people that support you following your desires.*

*What is one thing you want to do but feel like you need permission from someone else to do it?*

*Don't think about it. Trust the first thing that comes up.*

*Write it down.*

*Ask yourself, if I did have their permission, what's one thing I would do to move forward today?*

*Write it down.*

*How does it feel to think about having it?*

# I TOUCH MYSELF

There I was, lying on my mattress in my bare one-bedroom apartment with white walls. An apartment that I shared with my now ex-husband. In our relationship, and with myself, I had this increasing feeling that something was missing, and whatever *it* was, it was leaving a substantial and palpable void.

I was twenty-nine years old and naked, with the knowledge that I was about to do *it* for the first time, you know...touch myself.

I had all the necessary supplies with me. Next to me was a book on how to be multi-orgasmic that I had recently purchased which described a step-by-step massage that would end up...down there. I had the timer on my phone open and ready and...my hands.

It appeared I had everything I needed. To stall, I thought, "What else do I need? Perhaps a toy. Yes, woman, you need a vibrator or another book to make sure you do this right." I was searching for something to take longer to start this process. Luckily, a wiser part of me kicked in to remind me that I had everything I needed to do this. It was a moment of centering and refocus.

Just a moment later, I thought to myself, "I wish having an orgasm was as easy as receiving a birthday present. I'll take a nice juicy orgasm in a box, thank you very much."

...If it could only be that tangible.

Ugh.

The thing that drove me bonkers as I lay there was the nagging feeling that pleasure could partially be my responsibility or, God forbid, totally up to me. I laid on top of my comforter, feeling a bit chilly as I considered hiding under the covers to wrap myself up and somehow create a sense of more safety and comfort in this experience.

I laid on my back, addressing the job at hand. It certainly felt like work right now. I sternly said to myself, "You are going to touch yourself for ten minutes *and* you are going to like it!"

Right.

A part of me knew I needed to gently ease in with patience, but all that kept coming out of me was impatience and intolerance.

I glanced over to make sure that the blinds were closed and that there was no possible way that anyone could look in the window and see what I was doing. What would the neighbors think if they caught a glimpse somehow? How awkward would it be if I was touching myself and my husband walked in?

I hit start on the timer. I decided to use a timer because I kept avoiding this experience and needed some structure to get me started. I hoped that by hitting a "start" button, I would honor my commitment, at least until the buzzer went off.

Ladies and gentlemen, picture this for a moment. I was lying naked in my bed, looking back and forth between a book and my body, following each line like I was following a recipe.

I start at my head, and thought to myself, "that feels nice." I massaged my scalp, and I took an inhale followed by a long heavy exhale; the kind where I could hear my breath flowing out of my nostrils, and my jaw slightly relaxed.

"I can do this." This was a pep-talk-heavy exercise. You would think I was getting ready to run a race or tackle some intense and spectacular event that required great preparation as I psyched myself up, knowing that it was only going to get harder as I worked my way down south.

After massaging my scalp for a minute, I moved towards my neck. I felt a tickle as I gently drew my hands onto my shoulder, working down towards my collarbones. I felt like I was in the safe zone and could totally do this, until the suggestion: "Touch your breasts."

I cringed...

"Aww, hell no," came to mind as I wondered, "Is my body freaking out or my mind? What is the part of me that is so disgusted by this?" I felt like the task of finding pleasure in touching my breasts was synonymous to the Halloween game where there is a mystery object placed in a covered box, and it's up to me to feel inside blindly to identify what's in there.

I looked at the timer and only two minutes had passed. As angst rose up within me, I thought to myself, "Would the damn buzzer go off already so I can put this whole touching myself business off to the side until tomorrow when I designate another structured ten minutes to getting to the bottom of this?"

I justified that I had done enough already and went back and forth in my mind about shortening my ten-minute commitment to that of only two. I had already put in a lot of effort. I replayed all that I had done in my head, "I put my hands on my breasts and I squeezed them. I touched my nipples and circled my fingers around the outside. I mean, that's a big deal."

I gave myself a moment to breathe. I exhaled and decided that I could handle another eight minutes. What's the worst that could happen?

I ran my hands down my legs and my fingers found their way to kneading my upper thighs. As I continued to feel resistance, I wondered, "Is my body resisting feeling good about this, or is it the thoughts that keep popping into my mind telling me I'm doing something wrong that have a hold of me?" I was confused, to say the very least. Thoughts came into my mind that had been lying under the surface for years. They were telling me that the desire to touch my body was a ridiculous one.

I cringed again and squinted my eyes as I reached down

to touch the lips of my labia. I touched them with the anticipation that something either magical or horrible would happen with contact. I braced myself.

Turns out there were layers of skin there, like every other part of my body. *Well, that's not so bad.* It was neither horrible nor magical; in fact, it was quite anticlimactic. It tickled a bit and felt more sensitive than touching my arm, but I wasn't sure if that was just because I had never touched myself there before on purpose.

The book I had open to the side of me encouraged me to look at my genitalia, so I took the pocket mirror that I had placed by my side at the start of all of this, flipped it open, and positioned it so I could see my vagina and all its surrounding parts.

It was an interesting experience. There was a cross between wondering what the hell I was doing, accompanied by what I had to admit was relief. "They" were there, intact.

At this moment, I would like to note the fact that I have struggled many times over the years with what to call "them." Have you ever felt that naming your genitals feels strange or wrong, no matter what you call them? The vagina is only one part of my genitals, so I've heard that isn't even correct to say. Calling them "lady parts" or "down there" feels like a cop-out and juvenile. "Genitals" sounds impersonal and unsexy to me.

You'll see as you read on in this book, I have landed on the word "pussy." I have found it to be the most empowering word to describe my genitals. *Pussy* feels fun, light, feminine and a bit provocative. As you've read, and as you'll continue to read, what to call "them" has been a journey in itself.

In addition to my struggle over the proper name, as I lay there, I had nothing to compare *them* to visually. I gave myself a break when I saw an opening "down there." It felt like enough, and in that moment, I was satisfied with my findings. I felt confident I had what I needed to experience pleasure. It didn't appear that I was anatomically defective.

I spent about thirty seconds or so taking a look. Ladies and gents, if you have never taken a moment to look at your private parts, I would recommend it. It's a treat for the eyes and an opportunity for a perspective shift in the mind to look directly at a part of the body that is associated with so much emotional charge and subjective thinking.

Seeing our genitals directly, up close and personal, allows for a shift to happen. They hold a sacred space for incredible sensation and pleasure, and what houses all this possibility is just flesh. Skin, nerves, and the tissue that make us who we are.

Do I want to continue to be afraid of the possibilities held within this flesh I was born in?

I leaned back and touched myself for a couple of minutes. Breathing, trying to relax. Two minutes passed. I didn't have an orgasm. It felt awkward as hell to be touching myself. I was in limbo between the thoughts, "What's the big deal?" and "This is so new; we need to freak out," so I called it a day. "Let's try again another time," I told myself.

## THE WAKE UP

This one night of what I would like to call "brave action into unchartered waters" started me off on a stream of sleepless nights where I felt as though my mind and body were in an intense tug of war. It was a close battle with no winner in sight. It felt as though my body was begging me to touch it. My mind was acting as the militant gatekeeper, holding the impossible password and constantly changing it so that I would never get to the point of touching myself.

I would lie in bed, placing my hands on my belly, softly making their way down *there* and I would get just about to the point where I was going to touch my pussy, but I couldn't do it. Night after night this would happen, and the tension and frustration would continue to build.

One day, for no good reason at all, it hit me hard. This was no longer acceptable. It was like a part of me snapped, and I realized that from here on in I would be committed to getting to know my body.

It hit me that my approach from the first moment I touched myself was about a fight. In my head I was fighting my desire, I was fighting my resistance to the desire, and I was fighting my resistance to the resistance. Tiring just to think about, right?

There had to be another way. I was ready to stop fighting, at least for a moment. Fighting was raising the tension in my heart. I was fighting myself and trying to win the war by fighting harder. I wanted to let something happen that didn't feel like a battle, and I wasn't sure what that would look like.

I wondered: Could I find pleasure through listening to my body and desire? Could I give up the fight? Could I stop feeling so defensive and resistant?

I wanted to find out.

It turned out that one of the most powerful ways for me to give up the fight was to allow the fight. Interestingly enough, I discovered how to embrace my fight in a dark room with soft red lights placed in the corners. I'll introduce you to this dark room in the next chapter.

Before you do that though, let yourself be seen in the spark below. You are the only one looking! No one has to know.

SPARK

*Touch yourself. Set a timer for five minutes if you are new to it (and perhaps fifteen to twenty minutes for those that feel more confident).*

*Give yourself a massage from head to toe in a room where you will be undisturbed.*

*When you have judgements, take a moment to exhale, acknowledge them, and then continue. You might cringe; you might get excited. It's all good. Do it anyway.*

*For those that feel extra daring, have a pocket mirror handy as you start, and when you get to your genitals take out the mirror and look at them as you touch yourself.*

*What do you see, what do you notice? Colors, shapes, thoughts. Let it all be there.*

*If you do have a negative thought come up as you do this, say to it, "Thank you for sharing, but right now I am focusing on (and then direct yourself to something neutral that you are doing or observing)."*

*For example, say you have the thought, "You are disgusting," say to that thought, "Thanks for sharing, I hear you, but right now I am focusing on observing the colors of my labia."*

*Acknowledging the negative and bringing it back to*

*neutral is a helpful practice, as opposed to trying to push yourself through something that feels negative or beating yourself up even more for having negative thoughts. They come up. It's okay. Just bring yourself back when you notice it.*

# GETTING REAL WITH MYSELF

I was curled up in my cozy chair in the safety and silence of the corner of my room with my life coach on the other line reminding me of an essential truth.

"It's one thing to keep secrets from other people," he said, "but it's a very different and more painful thing to keep secrets from ourselves." As I sit now and reflect on how desire progresses, I remember that these are the worst kind of secrets. How much am I going to enjoy alone time if I haven't cultivated a relationship of honesty and trust with myself?

I can say I've played with this enough to know that the darker the room, the scarier the monsters appear. And the more I turn the light on, the more I get to see whether it's a furry teddy or a full-on grizzly bear that I've been afraid of. If I'm not willing to look at what I fear and at least see what it is, how will I ever learn how to work with and transform my relationship to it?

I went through a period where I had big secrets from

myself. I was trying to be bubbly and giggly and portray that I was a person who could continually take on more and more, but underneath, I wasn't. I was tired, hurt, angry, and I wasn't letting myself be any of those things. I wasn't really in a space of acknowledging it.

One Sunday night, I went out to dinner with a group of people, including one of the facilitators from a course on desire-based coaching I had been participating in. I was feeling exhausted from the day. I wanted to go home and get out of there, but I tried to push myself to stay engaged a bit longer and put on my best face. After we ordered our food, the instructor asked us to go around in a circle and to share how we were doing. When it came around to me, I shared something to the effect of, "I'm good," and forced a smile.

The instructor came closer to me and said, "I want you to tell me how you are really feeling, and I also want you to let yourself feel how you are really feeling." It took me a minute to sink and register what she said. When I *got it*, I took a breath and responded, "I'm feeling tired and a bit overwhelmed and run down." I didn't smile. I didn't try to sugarcoat it. I let myself feel the heaviness and weight I felt from my body.

And you know what? It was a massive relief. It felt awesome to be real with myself and others about where I was at. It has a huge "Aha!" moment for me.

This simple exercise of being true about my current state opened me up to a completely new way of relating to myself and others.

## LETTING THERE BE DRAMA

I was at a point where I wanted to be honest and let things be imperfect. I wanted permission to feel unhappy and frustrated, to not be fluffy happy all the time.

When I tried to force myself to be happy, I heard these voices: "What if I want to be a fucking mess right now? What if I *want* to be dramatic? What if all I care about is expressing myself authentically and worrying about how everything looks later?"

"I already know, for goodness' sake, I'm a good person, but what does that even mean anyway, and where has it gotten me? Has being good gotten me to a place of happiness and fulfillment? Or has it left me in a place where I'm urgently seeking another way?"

This dialogue helped me realize that I was desperate for a new way of being.

Desperation led me to a beautiful thing. Enter: the magic of sensual dance.

## THE ENTRANCE

I walked down the backstreet and stopped for a moment to look in both directions as I opened the heavy metal door which would lead me up to the school. I wanted to make sure no one was watching me walk in. I had this feeling that I was up to no good. It was conflicting yet titillating. The thought of being naughty and a "bad girl" popped into my mind, and it made me smile.

I made my way up the stairs. There was a spot at the door

to take off my shoes and socks so that I would walk into the room barefoot. The room was not well lit, in fact it was quite dark except for some lamps with red light bulbs which were placed in a few of the corners. There were no mirrors to be found.

I had lived in LA for about two months, and this studio had been one of the places that was first on my list to check out when I arrived. It felt important for me to go, so very shortly after settling in, I made my way to the studio.

A couple of weeks earlier, I had gone to the studio for an intro class. When I sat there watching the demo, I felt so nervous that I wanted to talk myself out of participating. A wiser part of me knew that I was there for a reason, and it encouraged me to sign up.

I laughed with disbelief at the teacher when she told those of us in the class that someday we would be doing what we were witnessing, which was a woman sensually pole dancing with a group of women watching her.

"Um, no. That will *not* be me," I declared to myself and the ladies next to me. "You think I'm going to do that?" I laughed to myself with a big "Hell no" on my mind, as I thought, "You don't know me! I would never be able to do that."

But alas, I did not leave, and I decided to give myself the benefit of the doubt that my frustrated and turned-off heart could be melted down into one that was gooey soft, hot, and open.

## FIRST CLASS

There I was, sitting on the purple mat. It was squishier than a regular yoga mat, yet about the same size. I was wearing a sports bra, tank top, and spandex running shorts. We were a class of all women sitting in a circle in this dimly lit space surrounded by a few cold, metal poles. I sat on the mat with faith that it would bring some form of liberation.

Goodness knows I had already spent too many days being wound up a little too tight. I teetered back and forth in my mind between, "This is awesome!" and "What the fuck are you doing?"

The teacher sat in the center with our mats positioned in a circle around her. Once we finished introducing ourselves, we were invited to drop our attention into our body and listen to the soft music as she guided us to move our bodies in multiple different circular motions. I felt clumsy, and it seemed impossible that I would get to a point where I would be able to get out of my head and enjoy my body the way that the instructor was recommending.

I could feel my muscles stretching and releasing tension as my mind struggled with a new type of movement which felt so much less goal-oriented than I was used to. We moved through a series of positions on the mat as music pulsed through the room. It was music that seemed to be coaxing a sensual part of me out into the room and soothed my body, forcing a break in my thoughts from time to time.

I kept hearing the teacher encouraging us to touch

ourselves, to let our hands run over our bodies, through the texture of our clothing, and to feel our skin as we brushed past it in the movement. It was the first time in my life I can recall someone encouraging me to touch myself in any kind of sensual manner. I was like, "What? Come again? You want me to do what?"

I thought to myself, "Is anyone looking? Is there anyone that can see what I'm about to do here? Can we make the lights a little darker please?" The crazy thing is, she was doing more than just encouraging me to touch myself. She was also giving me permission to find pleasure in it. To indulge and linger.

A part of me wanted to be like, "Woman, do you know we are in a public place? You want me to touch myself with other people around me who can see what I'm doing?" A massive "hell no" came to mind once again.

This "hell no" reaction seems to happen to me when I'm on the verge of something great. Funny, right? Another of the many fascinating and beautiful paradoxes of this life. I've learned that the moments when I follow an inspiration and then shortly afterwards feel scared to death, those are the moments when it's often in my best interest to trust myself to keep moving forward.

Thankfully another part of me was thinking I paid for this, and it might be worth taking a moment to slow myself down enough to try. I closed my eyes and let myself sink into the feeling.

I am grateful that I slowed down. I'm grateful that I started to touch my body in sensual ways and learned to tune into it because it began to connect me with my ability to have more. And this is what was intriguing to me. I could feel a thawing out of my body and the fade of my frigidity.

I was letting my movements be slower. I was touching myself. I was letting myself feel more. Initially, I would leave class feeling exhausted after two hours on a Saturday morning and feel worn out for the rest of the weekend. This new way of relating to my body felt like a shock to my system.

As the weeks progressed, this run down feeling began to shift, and the classes started to feed me more as I started to leave with more energy than I walked in with. To this day, going to class always feeds me and nourishes me. I leave feeling like I have been seen and heard and expressed.

It didn't take long for me to see the value of feeling not just the pretty stuff like love, happiness, and joy. I saw how feeling the dark stuff like sadness and anger was fueling and tremendously powerful. In this playground, I was encouraged to let it all have a place.

I was having some of my first experiences with alchemy. I was over the shit of pretending I was always okay. I had feelings, dark feelings. I started to discover a more primal part of myself, a part that liked dark, dirty music and that wanted to throw tantrums.

My usual behavior for a large part of my life was showing my best front out in public, but shutting down in private and home settings when I wasn't happy. I didn't know what to do when I felt upset, so I wouldn't do anything except isolate myself. It was easy for those close to me to see I was upset, but not so easy to find resolution because I often wouldn't communicate what was happening inside of me.

Dancing taught me to feel my typically pent-up emotions without rethinking and rehashing them. I let the emotions flow through me and have their moment through my movements by dropping out of my mind and into my body. If I felt the charge or sensation of them in my body, they didn't hold so much power over me in my mind. I was clearing some emotional charge from whatever was on my mind so I could think about it more objectively.

There are many moments where my body can say far more eloquently what my lips struggle to express. Oftentimes when I am emotionally triggered, my words can seem incomplete and secondary to something that calls to physically move through me first. So, I let myself move until I feel a shift in the emotional charge, and then I see how I want to respond.

## SEXY CAME SECOND

I'd love to say my sexy came flowing out of me with ease and grace. The truth is that before anything else, my anger, hurt, sadness, and unapologetic feisty-self wanted a place to speak. My body found its bliss through expression of those feelings moving to songs like *Counting Bodies Like Sheep to the Rhythm of the War Drums* and *Killing in the Name*.

There were moments of sexy, naughty playfulness weaved in, but this heaviness and darkness had its voice before the more joyful sassiness woke up.

The beauty of schools that create structure and containers for emotional transformation through movement is that the darkness is expressed in a safe and protected space as free from judgment and harm as possible. I can be anything in that space, and it will be honored.

I was learning to give myself the gift of alchemy; a way of expressing pain that let me move through and onwards instead of lugging it on my back as another burden to bear and carry with me.

In doing this practice, I realized that when I allow and express the messy, "out of control" parts of me, they bring me together and help me feel more in control.

The incredible lesson I learned from these classes and from the coaches I worked with during this time is that it's okay to be where I am emotionally. If I am sad, let myself be sad. If I have anger or fear, feel them and let them be seen instead of trying to show the face of joy all the time.

It's taken me a while to see that being real about my anger, for example, doesn't mean I'm complaining or being a burden or going to be labeled as emotional. Others might judge me as those things, and I'll probably judge others as those things from time to time. That's not the point. Having emotions is human. I'll move through them a lot faster and learn from it if I honor it.

How we express ourselves in response to our experiences gets better through practice and by being willing to try. The act of trying is its own perfection.

Release the pressure to feel like you have to present yourself in a pretty little box to everyone you meet. Tell yourself the truth. Let it be dark and honest, and then you can figure out what you want to do from there. Find a safe place for these parts of yourself. I highly recommend that one of those spaces be a place for sensual movement.

The thought of this might make you excited, or it might make you want to hide away, which brings me to my next lesson: You'll do it when you're ready. There is no wrong way to live out desire. You will get there one way or another. The more you show your desire that you are loyal to it, the more it will remind you of its presence.

# SPARK

*Ask yourself, "How do I feel right now?" If you struggle to grasp a word, some emotions are: sadness, joy, fear, anger, surprise and disgust. Find a song that matches that mood. Trust what pops into your mind and put it on.*

*Dance how you feel. If it's light and airy, hop and skip around the room. If it's heavy, maybe you start in a push-up position and feel every ounce of tension or weight in your body as you move.*

*Let it be real. Have fun with it and practice slipping back into your body throughout the song. You will probably go back and forth between being in your thoughts and being in your body. Each time you realize you are judging your movement, drop yourself back down into your body and put your attention into your body. Start with a flick of your wrist or a circle of your hips. The idea here is to let this be a body experience.*

*Once the song is over, check in with yourself to see if you feel a shift in your mental or emotional state. Does your body feel any different than when you started? Perhaps lighter or more alive?*

## I'LL DO IT WHEN I'M READY

These words have become one of my favorite mantras, "I'll do it when I'm ready."

As I went to my weekly pole dancing classes, I learned that some days I would feel amazing, some days I would be in a tug of war with myself with no sign of surrender on either side, and some days I would feel utterly out of control and there would be nothing much I could or would want to do about it.

Part of learning to feel good requires learning to feel, period. To feel everything, including the resistance.

When I resist something, I don't want to feel or resist the fact that I am resisting, I enter into a resistfest at Stuckville. It's not a pretty place to be. I feel like I'm not acting fast enough, and the more I feel I am not acting fast enough, the more I feel like I'm moving in quicksand. It feels awful and empty. Ugh, it's sexless, lifeless, and void of everything but blah-ness and fury.

I've had plenty of days where there is fury moving

through me, and it feels so gratifying to do the slowest push-ups humanly possible to feel every ounce of heaviness and irritation in my body. I've learned that if I don't put my angst into my muscles and take it out of my head, that some poor innocent soul, most likely my man, will unnecessarily pay a price.

When I let my experience of life feel heavy in my pelvis or foggy in my head, if that is my truth at a given moment, it actually feels true and perfect. When I don't let myself be where I am at, it doesn't feel right in my body.

Some days I pick the dirtiest, sexiest song on my playlist that possesses my hips with the desire to grind. There is nothing better than the desire and sensation to let my hips grind as if they were going for the center of the earth. I love those days.

Other weeks I reach for Ed Sheeran's *Give Me Love*, inviting me to drip my hands slowly over every curve of my body feeling the texture and temperature of my skin.

Pole dancing and sensual movement has become my ultimate place for expression, my therapy, emotional release, exercise, and place to process. I see that the more I just let it be, whatever "it" is on any given day, the faster I move through it.

Some days I am ready for the next thing, and some days I'm not. And I'm not ready until I am. That's just the way it is.

## THE INTRODUCTION

One day at the end of class, I heard some of the other ladies talking about something called a Pole Dancing Amateur Night. It was a place where everyday women had the opportunity to pole dance at a real strip club for a crowd of men and women. Yup, the general public.

There would be no more safety of a classroom full of supportive women, and there was no affiliation with the studio where I went to class. These events were open to anyone that wanted to walk in, witness, and throw dollar bills out at the women dancing. A part of me was curious about it, but another part of me was still thinking, "No way. There is no way I can do that."

In class, I did notice that being watched felt great. I would get extremely nervous when I knew I would be watched, but when the music came on, a switch went off inside of me, and I was ready.

I often get a bit nervous when I am about to be witnessed, but as I start to dance, the butterflies often transform into fuel for my movement. My body knows what to do, and most of the time I enter a blissful state of being witnessed.

I had gone from dancing in a dark room, unable to open my eyes, to being able to have my eyes open and look at the other fabulous women I was dancing with. I was even able to make eye contact with them. I had come so far, but going to a place where I would be on a stage and both men and women would be watching me was a whole other ball game.

I wasn't ready.

I was intimidated by the idea of it all, but curiosity lingered. This was not the first time I had taken this approach. I dip a toe, I dip a toe...possibly dip the toe in one to fifteen more times, and then I jump. I've accepted that sometimes this is the way I do things. I'm not ready until I am. I will pay attention on the outskirts to what people are doing that I want to do, I'll soak in what they are saying and experiencing, and when I'm ready, I'll do it.

I find peace in knowing that, "I'm not ready now," in no way means, "I won't be ready forever." It means, "I'm not quite there yet, and it's all good."

This is how it went down with the amateur night. One day I simply decided I was ready. I had heard enough women talking about it, and I could feel some envy and jealousy arising inside of me. I wanted what they were having. It looked so satisfying.

I remember being out with a friend shopping for cute little knick-knacks, probably with some inspirational quote, to put somewhere. When I told her, she was so excited for me, she knew how much fun I was having exploring this part of myself and has been one of my biggest cheerleaders over the years.

It felt surreal to acknowledge to a friend that I was going to get on a stage at a strip club open to the public, and that I would dance for money. Well, kind of...that wasn't the reason I was doing it, but that would be part of the result. The idea of having money thrown at me did sound enticing. "I'll take some of that," I thought.

Of course I had doubts that I would walk off the stage

empty-handed. Maybe no one would throw money out for me? *Uh oh.* Fear crept in. That would stink. I decided to only share the event details with a few friends I knew would be supportive, including my fellow classmates. This felt like a big desire for me. I was on the sensitive side about it and hesitant to share with many people in my social network.

## THE WARM-UP

As a warm-up, I volunteered at this monthly event to clean the poles before my scheduled date to get a feel for the experience. I wanted to get my feet wet by watching other women perform, up close and personal. In between their dances I would rag down the poles to prepare them for the next dancer.

I was asked to dress in all black. I decided on a black bra, black panties, and a black see-through, skin-tight, long-sleeve mesh dress that barely covered my booty. Nothing I would have been seen wearing in public on any day of the week outside of this forum, *ever*.

I wore a pair of thigh-high leather boots for two reasons. One, because they were sexy and I felt fabulous in them. Two, I heard my legs could get beat up and tired from going up and down the pole all night, and the leather would stick to the pole and make it easier as the night progressed.

It might not look like it as women go up and down a pole, but as sexy as it looks, pole dancing can very easily lead to a body full of bruises. Remember, she's on a steel metal pole. Bruises come with the territory. But please don't let this deter you if you have wanted to try it. Signing up for a class was one of the best decisions I have made.

As I walked into the club, I stood in front of a proper pole dancing stage with an elevated runway and two poles on either end. There was a front row of seats which bordered the runway, along with white lights to indicate where the action was at.

It was fun to think about witnessing other women dance, and the thought that just maybe I was possibly being watched as I wiped down the poles in my lingerie left me full of joyful anticipation. I fully intended not to dance and to soak it all in as a spectator.

I was taken aback when the organizer came over to me and gave me the offer to get up there and dance that first night I came to volunteer. They were down a dancer that night, so I was asked if I'd like to get up there. I said yes. What the hell, right? I made it this far!

Now, mind you, I didn't say yes right away.

I said, "Let me think about it."

She responded, "You have five minutes."

I paced. I peed. I thought, "Fuck it, no one here really knows me anyway. Let's do this."

It was so incredibly foreign to be dressed in sexy, revealing clothing. It was a cross between feeling like a fish out of water awkwardly floundering around in high heeled boots and a feeling that I had just liberated myself by stripping off layers, literally and symbolically, to let myself feel and be in a state of sexual, sassy, feisty *woman*.

When it was my turn, Ne-Yo's *She Knows* came through the speakers. I felt a moment of paralysis and a flurry of sensation surging through my body from my pussy all the way up to my head. I started with my hands on the pole to breathe and ground myself as I felt all eyes on me. I took a nice long exhale and let one of my curves lead the movement as I had been taught in class. After a few seconds, my body took over. It became a glorious blur.

When I am dancing, my body often takes over. Every single part of me has a stage to be expressed, and it's all welcome: the bitch, the slut, the innocent good girl, and the hard worker, to name a few. The parts of me that crave your attention, that want to hide away, or that will stare you down like she could eat you alive if she wanted to, can all be present. All of me has a place and it's incredibly fueling.

## THE BIG NIGHT

There is an exhibitionist in me that is very alive and well, and she loves to play. I felt it as I cleaned the poles that night I volunteered, and I felt it even more when I performed as scheduled a couple months later and had the full experience for myself of carefully choosing the sexy outfits I wanted and the songs that I felt would most awaken my fun, primal side and erotic side.

The crowd was full of friends, family, and strangers of the performers. I enjoyed the thought that those who knew me were there to share their love, but was equally excited by the idea of someone watching me who knew nothing about me. It was titillating to think that someone who didn't even know my name could be fantasizing about what they would like to do with me.

As I was getting ready that day, it felt like I was back in high school or college the day of a cross-country race, barely able to eat as the adrenaline ran through me. I was stretching on and off all day and going pee every thirty seconds as it got closer. I became quiet as my time to dance approached; I wanted to get into the zone.

I've always considered myself a fan of the underdog and the one who humbly surprises, so I liked the idea of being lo-pro about it all. It was impossible to know how it would look to anyone else anyway, so the most I could do was make sure it felt as good as possible.

I remember that night after dancing, I found it impossible to go back to sleep. I lay in bed feeling like I had run a marathon. My knees were bruised, my lower back ached, but my heart was full and my wallet had an extra $150 bucks. I was impressed with what I had done as I thought back to the time where I was nervous even to try a class.

I got up on that stage and let myself move in a way that felt fierce and sexy. I played with eye contact and did tricks where I went upside down on the pole. I got to showcase my physical strength and the way my body naturally expressed sexy. I had fun, and it felt incredible. There were moments where I forgot where I was and left behind who I was beyond the moment.

I learned through this whole experience not to fret when I wasn't ready for something, to trust if I had desire, and to let it all play out. If I feel a call, I keep my eyes open for the smaller steps I am willing to take.

# SPARK

*What's one thing you've been wanting to do, but you don't feel ready?*

*Take a little time to research it. Find out who is doing it, how they are doing it, what their experience is with it, and see if that sparks a deeper interest or leads to your desire fizzling out.*

*This is something I love about research—it's still forward movement. It's enough that you can gather more information to make a decision, but it's safer than putting yourself into a new experience when the fear factor might be too high.*

# NOT EVERYONE WILL LIKE IT

When I danced at the amateur night, I wanted to have pictures of the experience to take forward with me to remember this night of feeling like a sexy badass. The woman who ran the event had a photographer present for those who wanted a package of photos, and I was definitely one of them. Years later, I still have one of the photos from that night on my bedroom wall.

I learned from sharing about that night that on the path to pleasure there will be opposition if I start sharing my excitement and experiences of sexual liberation with others. The more I have "gone for it" so to speak, the more I know who gets it and who doesn't. I've learned that talking about sex can trigger all kinds of discomfort for people, and there are some that don't want anything to do with the conversation.

I know this probably sounds like a no-brainer as you read this, but this was, and still is at times, a tough lesson for me. Sometimes I still hope that somehow if I have enough passion for something I will be able to get everyone on board with me.

When I got my photos back from the evening, there was one in particular that lit me up so incredibly that I felt compelled to share it with the world on Facebook. I wanted to shout from the rooftops what an incredible experience it was and how I wished for every woman to have the feeling of taking a stand for their sexuality, beauty, and unapologetic expression.

I thought about whether or not I wanted to post it for over a week. On the one hand, it was controversial for me. It was pole dancing at an actual strip club. What would people think of me? On the other hand, I was high from the experience and felt compelled, enthusiastic, and overjoyed in a way that I couldn't contain. What's more, I didn't want to contain it.

I decided my feelings of empowerment outweighed the judgement of any bystanders. I posted a picture of myself in movement on my hands and knees with my long curly dark brown hair covering my face, my lips just slightly opened and my gaze in the direction of one of my friends. A leg dressed in fishnet stockings was raised with red lingerie trailing off my body at my upper thigh. The essence of my unapologetic expression of sexual and sensual bliss was captured.

The posted picture was a celebration and a way to say, "Hey people! Have some of what I'm having; it's so good!"

As I hit send, I braced myself for what might come next.

This was a bit of an uncharacteristic post for me. I had no idea what to expect.

Some of the women I danced with shared their love and I felt supported, which left me with the warm fuzzies. *And*, I got some unexpected private messages from people close to me that I love and respect telling me that I should be careful what I post on social media if I want to be respected as a business owner someday (which was something I was actively working towards).

I had people close to me tell me that they asked their families to unfriend me on Facebook because they felt that my post was inappropriate. I was also hearing that people who knew me but no longer lived close to me were gossiping that something must have happened to me, that I used to be a "good girl."

I was disheartened for quite a while about this, wondering what I could do to convince them of the impact it had on my life, and then I realized that none of them actually reached out to me to say, "Hey, it sounds like this is something you are really excited about. Tell me more."

They didn't want to be in a conversation with me about what I was up to, so why was I stressing so much about getting them to understand how great it all was? They weren't my audience; they weren't my support system. It was time to let go of wanting to convince them to be.

One of the hardest things for me to hear was that I heard through the grapevine that people said I was no longer a "good girl." Although the part of me that is happy about my road to sexual liberation has fun with being a "bad girl," two things made me very unhappy about these comments.

One was that I genuinely care about being a good person. Being respectful, kind, and supportive is something I pride myself on. How could my "good girl" card be taken away with one picture? It felt unfair.

I also felt quite disappointed for the lack of progress in the realm of acceptance of sexual expression. Why, on a broader scale, do we label people in a judging manner as to whether they are good and bad based on their consensual sexual activity and expression?

I'm all about playfully being a bad girl in the bedroom, but when someone talks down to me because I want to let my sex out, I have those moments where I doubt myself and have to ask, "Is this really okay? Can I be that sexual? Can I let that part of myself be seen?"

The answers I keep coming back to time and time again, are yes, yes, and yes.

Letting myself be fully expressed sexually goes beyond the battle of good vs bad girl status. It is about embracing my natural state and following desire. It's about leaning into what feels amazing and alive in my skin and letting that fuel me for life.

If someone doesn't want to hear it, they aren't going to listen. It's not worth trying to explain my love to an ear that has shut down. It's worth making peace with the fact that they aren't the ones who I share this part of myself with at this time.

As I was getting ready to publish this book, I was asked if

I would consider writing it anonymously by a few people that were nervous for me and thought the book could possibly lead to a tainted reputation. That would be defeating the purpose. How can I say I want to be a voice for sexual liberation and expression, yet not put my name on it? I'd be a hypocrite by basically saying, "You should totally go for it! But I'm a little too nervous about what others might think. So I'm going to keep it quiet."

I will never make everyone happy. You, my beautiful and fabulous friend, will never make everyone happy, and our paths may never be met by all those we love. If we follow our desires and do what makes us happy, it is inevitable that we will be letting someone down. And that is okay.

It's becoming increasingly clear that desire doesn't care what we look like in the eyes of others, and it doesn't entirely care where we are right now. Desire, in my experience, is about setting new paths for myself and pushing boundaries of what I thought was possible. Sometimes it can be born out of joyful desire, and sometimes it's out of necessity.

# SPARK

*Put your hand on your heart and say to yourself, "I will never make everyone happy, and that's okay. I'm here to find out what makes me happy."*

*Notice what happens in your body when you do that. And in your mind.*

*Is it hard to say or hear? Or does it bring with it a sigh of relief? Or perhaps it brings both.*

*Repeat, repeat, and repeat this one if you are a people-pleaser.*

## FINDING STRENGTH THROUGH
## FEELING SEXY

When I got divorced, I didn't know where I was going to get the strength to do it. It is not easy to end a marriage. There were years where I heavily judged those who divorced, but I have learned that sometimes it really is the best thing.

It doesn't even matter whose fault it is anymore; it just has to be done because the relationship isn't working. In the case of my divorce, I believe we both felt we did everything we could and that, as a team, we had died.

I tried more than once in my head to tell myself I was going to end it. He wasn't abusive, neither one of us was, but it wasn't working. We had both tried, and I had nothing left. I did everything I knew at the time to save it, but I had reached my point of no return.

I remember the moment when I knew it. I was sitting outside of dance class and tears started to stream down my face. It hit me that it was over, and I felt a void as I realized the amount of change it would require for me to follow through.

I started to think about all the ways that we were tangled financially and emotionally and how all of that would need to be unraveled. Separating bills, new bank accounts, an empty bed, and uncomfortable conversations about how it was really over and when and how he would leave.

I wondered where I was going to get the energy and the umph to follow through with ending it when he still wanted to work it out. This is where I started to learn that tapping into feeling sexy can help me find strength.

An old co-worker and Facebook friend, Jeff, reached out after seeing pictures of me from my amateur night adventures. There have been a few instances where men from my past have reached out after seeing pole dancing pictures thinking that somehow it was going to line them up with a better chance at having a night in bed with me. This was one of those moments.

Jeff took an interest in my dancing, which made me feel wanted and feisty. This old friend was flattering and complementary, and I let myself take it all in. Our interactions gave me fuel to keep going with my divorce. It gave me strength in a time where I felt lost as to how we would end things and find resolution.

Jeff was younger than I was. He was cute and had more of a rugged feel to him than my husband. He also had more of a naughty innocence, which provoked another side of me to come out. It gave me a much-needed break from the organized, structured, and down to business part of myself that was getting overworked. Our interactions made me feel sexy, wanted, vibrant, and young.

His compliments and desire to see me dance weren't the only thing I got from my connection with him. He was my first experience with sexting. Some may say this was cheating because I didn't yet have divorce papers in my hands. Maybe it was, but in my head and heart the marriage was over, and I needed strength to end it.

If it works, it works, and in this moment I needed to do something to build up the reserve to get through this. I knew trying to run on fumes would not last me. He, this, whatever we were doing...was working. It was fueling me.

There were a couple times where Jeff and I created a scene and elaborated on it...a snowy winter night in a Jacuzzi where he was kissing my neck and running his fingers through my hair. I loved the story and the build. It fired me up and left me wanting more. It brought fun and possibility back into my life.

I was actually using my imagination, which had felt pretty shut down for quite some time. He wanted to see me dancing, so I created home videos from my pole at home where I would do a little strip tease to songs I loved. A few I sent, but I also kept a few and relished in seeing myself move in a way that brought me such bliss.

I remember there was probably a month straight where I played the song *All The Time* by Jeremih on repeat. It repeats many times over, "I could fuck you all the time," with the background of a slow R&B style sound. Mm, good. It was heavenly for me during that period of time. It was the kind of slow, sexy grounding that my body needed when I would get lost in my head about all the worries of the future.

When I looked back months later, I found that a patch of my hair about the size of a tennis ball had fallen out from stress and I was fifteen pounds lighter without trying. The marriage, the divorce, all of it, took a lot out of me over time.

The adrenaline I had flowing through me and the fumes I was living on were what got me through. I believe those fumes came from connecting to this sexy and sensual part of myself which felt completely untapped most of the time.

This was the beginning of a deeper dive into what made me feel sexy, and I started making the association that feeling sexy and being sexual gave me energy. I realized how, without even being touched physically by another, I could feel sexier. I never knew I could be so turned on by a sexy picture being painted for me in my head.

I have experimented with many different ways to feel sexy since that day, ranging from wearing sexy undies or lingerie, to putting on a tasty colorful lip gloss, to even wearing a pearl thong at work just to see how it would feel.

I will warn against the pearl thong at work; it's a horrible idea, really.

Have you ever worn a pearl thong? They look a hell of a lot sexier than they feel. You know the little spaces between the pearls? They bite. And when they are up against the most sensitive part of your body, rubbing against your clitoris and your labia. *Wow*. It's *not* comfortable. It was hilarious and painful. I had to go to the bathroom and move the string of pearls all the way to the outer side of the lip of my labia in order to make it through the day. I just couldn't bring myself to take them off. It was too much fun to know I was wearing them.

There are so many ways to feel sexy and remind yourself of the fact that you are a sexual being. You are. I promise you! And if you picked up this book, you know it. So play with embodying it.

A fabulous way to play with letting new and sexy in is to welcome what is different into your life. In the next chapter, I'll share how doing some of the things we never thought we would do are not only our greatest teachers, they are some of the best ways to spark desire.

# SPARK

*What connects you with feeling sexy and being sexual?*

*Is it wearing something particular? Is it sexting with a special friend? Is it finding ways to flirt during the day or complimenting strangers as you pass them in the street?*

*Is it lying back and imaging yourself in an erotic circumstance with the man or woman of your dreams? Is it simply a lip gloss or particular robe you wear at the end of the day to unwind?*

*If you are stuck, try the prompt: "I feel sexy when...." and see what comes up. Set a timer for five minutes, and continue to write down this prompt and the inspiration that follows.*

*Do this not just when you are happy and everything is going smoothly, but when times are hard. When times are hard and you are tired, you'll want to forget about this. I encourage you to stay in touch with desire and your body whether you feel like it or not.*

*I bet you'll find you are glad you did.*

# WELCOME DIFFERENT

I started dating a few months after the divorce process started with my ex. It happened by accident more than anything else. I found myself in judgment when I thought about how much time I should be spending taking a break from dating and sex after a divorce, but since when is anything ever a straight line?

I have learned that feeling good and focusing on what I want is not a linear process and trying to force it into one will only leave me feeling more frustrated.

## THE SWEET ENCOUNTER

It was a moment of sweet serendipity when I walked into the coffee shop he was managing on a cool December night. My friend and I walked in, ready to sit down for a nice long catch-up over a cup of tea after a few months of not seeing each other. We planned to go somewhere else entirely, but as she was driving, I asked her to redirect to a

JACLYN LACEY FOSTER

super cute coffee shop on the outskirts of Los Angeles that I had only been to once or twice before.

When we walked up to order our drinks, David and I made eye contact. I immediately felt the chemistry, and my heart fluttered in my chest as my throat went dry. As we smiled at each other and connected with playful eye contact, he let me know the peppermint tea I was ordering was organic and in unison we both responded, "Even better."

My friend and I walked outside and sat down to enjoy our drinks. David made three trips out to our table, making small talk and taking care of business around me. To my surprise, but very much meeting the prediction of my friend, he asked me if I wanted to go out country line dancing sometime and offered to give me a slice of his family's famous homemade lasagna.

I didn't have the heart to tell him at the time that I wasn't eating dairy. The gesture was kind and unique, and I was intrigued. I gave him my number, and when he texted and asked me out a couple days later, we made plans to meet up the following Friday.

We went bowling, something I have always loved to do. I have fond memories of going to the bowling alley as a child with my parents when they played in a league. We would run around the alley playing pool and video games as we heard the clunking of the pins in the background.

David and I, as we found out, were complete opposites in some ways.

He is a smoking meat-eater who is eager to speak his mind and share his opinion. Sometimes I laugh as he seems to see it as his moral obligation to be as honest as possible at all times, regardless of how others feel about it. Often he will say what's on his mind first, just letting it out and then afterwards will take the time to think about whether or not there are any consequences to what he just said.

I was a plant-based non-smoker who was overly careful to not offend anyone with the hope and belief that somehow I could live a life where I would please or be on good terms with everyone I met for the rest of my life. I was, and still am, very nice, but I was so nice that I often bent over backwards to help people and was a bit of a doormat at times.

We were both in a time of transition in our lives for different reasons. His mother was reaching the end of her life, and he was caring for her as I was in the middle of a divorce. I remember on the first date he shared that he could see himself with me for a long time. We sat in my blue Toyota Yaris, me in the driver seat and him as my passenger, not wanting the night to end.

To add to our difference, we had very different views and experience levels when it came to sex. He started having sex quite a bit younger than I did, and he had a much lighter attitude around it. For him, it was something fun. He enjoyed variety and had been in relationships that involved a level of non-monogamy. I had not.

I had only known monogamy and was kind of excited and a little scared of the fact that there was something possible beyond that. I wanted to dip a toe in those waters but had no idea what I was doing.

It became an incredible gift knowing someone that was so

willing to unapologetically be himself, a lesson I was (well, if I'm being honest with myself, *am*) still coming to learn. Different can be okay, heck...different can be amazing. It can be an incredible teacher, lover, and partner.

Without letting someone into my life that was so different from me, I would not be the woman I am today. As a result of our differences, we have both expanded our perspectives and, I would dare say, are more open, accepting, and better people as a result.

I have learned to have a stronger voice, to share my opinions with no or less apology. I have some red meat a couple times a month, and I have an incredibly different perspective on my relationship to sex now. I see it as something that is fun and for pleasure in a way that I was closed off to before him.

I won't speak for him, but I know he sees that being with me has benefitted him. Much of it is due to our differences and our commitment to communicating through it all and expanding our abilities to see each other's perspective.

Now I'm not saying that your version of different has to mean needing a partner who is your opposite, but I am asking, what if you explored a relationship, an activity, a class that was the opposite of what you are used to? Perhaps something that is opposite of what a good girl would do?

# SPARK

*Who or what in your life intrigues you or draws your attention in that it would be the complete opposite of something you would typically do?*

*Give yourself the opportunity to explore it.*

*If it's a person, invite them out to coffee to learn more about them. If it's an activity, sign up for a class.*

*Try it, or them, a few times and see if it gets you excited or expands your view of what is possible or of who you are.*

# BE WILLING TO RECEIVE

It's called OM for short. Orgasmic Meditation,[1] that is. I looked into it while I was still married, and my ex didn't want to do it. At the time, I didn't feel comfortable with going ahead and doing it without him and I didn't have the fire in me to push back when he said no. It felt too provocative.

A few months after we separated, life started to feel like it was moving in new directions very quickly. I knew it was time to try this practice, and I knew from my research the first step was something called a TurnOn.

A TurnOn is an in-person event where three communication exercises are practiced in a group environment. I knew the Orgasmic Meditation practice required a woman to take her pants off and be half naked, but it looked like this event would be fully clothed and just oral. You know oral, like speaking. Not oral, like sex. That's an idea though, right?

I was feeling very energized by this sexual side of me

waking up. I wanted to feel it more and this was just the thing.

In hindsight, I know that I was yearning for two things: genuine connection and to receive with "exquisite attention," as I heard it called. But in the moment, I was just hungry to embrace sex. I know that's general, but I wanted a better relationship to sex. Period.

After the communication exercises, I signed up for a full day class where I learned the basics of OM, a 15-minute consciousness practice where a person (man or woman) strokes a woman's clitoris in a structured environment.

I learned that this was a practice about receiving and focusing on feeling and a place where the need for compensation was left at the door. Both partners were to participate knowing that the whole purpose was to feel for their own pleasure and put their focused attention on the stroke of the clitoris. Nothing more, nothing less.

At the end of this one-day course, I was going to have the opportunity to try the practice myself. I was going to have my clitoris stroked by someone in that very room, someone I most likely hadn't even spoken with for more than five minutes. He was going to keep his pants on. I was going to be taking mine off.

When we got to *that time,* a number of us women were in the bathroom deciding whether or not we were going to follow through with it. It was a feeling like being at the school dance and nervously awaiting a dance with one of the boys.

When we emerged, laid out awaiting us were "nests" which included a set of blankets and pillows to practice on. I remember lying down, thinking that my partner was someone I never thought I would take my clothes off in front of in a million years. I didn't consider him to be "my type." I've learned that finding *my type* is not what a practice like this is about. It's about feeling into whatever is happening instead of sticking to my preconceived idea of what I should like or have liked in the past.

As I laid down with my pants off half naked and my legs butterflied open, my partner sat over me and was instructed through the steps of the practice and guided as to how to stroke my clitoris. I could feel myself bracing. I reminded myself to breathe and felt conflicted about whether or not I was willing to relax into it or if it was best to keep my guard up, ready to crush the hand that goes out of line.

I couldn't decide.

More than anything, it was awkward as we struggled to find a groove together. He was nervous, just as I was, and we were in a room full of other people doing the same thing. I could give him adjustments if I wanted him to change the amount of pressure or location of his stroking on my clitoris. In the moment I decided I would save my adjustments for another day, there was a lot going on and we were both taking in a very new and foreign experience.

Although it was more awkward than sexually arousing, I couldn't help but feel liberated about it. It was a step towards knowing myself better and letting myself be touched in a way that I hadn't experienced before.

When we both sat up after the practice, it was a weird

moment where both of us knew this was not a date and we weren't leaving together, but yet we shared something intimate. The staff did a great job of helping us transition through the steps. We ended up exchanging information so that we could do the practice again another time.

*I will say that I believe OneTaste no longer includes the part during the Intro class where you get to practice with someone, but there are plenty of resources to get started with this practice. In the resources at the end of this book I share their website and the founder, Nicole Daedone's, book, where I first became intrigued with and started learning about the practice.*

## THE CHOICE TO STAY TRUE

I was intrigued enough from that day forward to start OMing as they call it, regularly. It took me a while to build up any kind of proper regularity with it all, but I made the decision to keep it up. David on the other hand, who I was getting more serious with, was not a fan of the practice, and it became of a point of contention for us.

It feels funny to me that my journey into OM started the morning after my first date with David. I feel like the universe might have presented me with both David and OM at the same time to help me stay balanced, honest, and true to myself.

One of the most amazing things I get and continue to get from this practice is a place where my only job is to receive. It's a space where my "job" so to speak, is to feel.

I have to continually decide if it is worth making the time to receive, because sometimes David wants to do the practice and sometimes he doesn't. Sometimes he's fine with me doing it with someone else and sometimes he isn't. But regardless of how he is processing it on any given day, we have an agreement that this is a practice that is important to me. We are clear on this, and I do it.

I have to choose to focus on how I am going to respond to his enthusiasm or lack of enthusiasm and of course how I will respond to my own.

It is such a massive relief some days to know I have a place like that with no obligation. I am positive that having this forum has led me to being able to experience more pleasure and to give myself permission to expand my desires.

Receiving without need for compensation is crucial to living a life that feels sustainably good. A life that is always focusing on repaying someone for something or keeping tabs is just plain icky and unsustainable.

Years ago, if someone got me a gift or did something nice for me, I would file it away in my brain as something I had to repay *soon*. Just the other day, a friend of mine bought me a gift of these intuitive cards that I love to play with whenever I am at her home. She thought of me when she saw them and got them for me. I had a moment as I opened the perfectly wrapped golden paper and thought, "Oh goodness, I don't have anything for her."

Then I took a moment, slowed down, and realized that is not what this is about. This is about receiving something that a friend of mine wanted me to have. *Receive it.* I opened it up with so much joy and then we christened the card set together as we each picked a card, read it, and reflected on its significance. It felt amazing to hold them in my hands, and I was so touched that she thought to get them for me.

I let myself receive them.

If a friend wants to take you out to dinner, what about letting them do it? If your partner goes to give you a hug after you've been distant for a while, what if you let yourself have that gift of touch? If your partner is going down on you, can you feel it and let yourself take it in without thinking about what you have to do next for them?

If you want pleasure, you've got to practice receiving. Whether it be a compliment or a kind gesture. Take it in with a "Thank you." Receive, receive, and receive. I can't tell you enough how important this one is. It truly takes practice to do this gracefully, but it is well worth the practice.

ENDNOTE

[1] Orgasmic Meditation is a trademark of OneTaste and is used with their permission.

# SPARK

*What is a place or time in your life where your only task is to receive?*

*How does it feel when you are receiving? Are you looking for ways to repay the person as you are receiving or are you soaking it in?*

*If you don't have a sacred place like this, ask for it. You can ask a partner, a friend, a group or community. You can ask for a hug, an ear to listen, an OM, or oral sex, to name a few. If you receive a "yes," practice taking it in by being as present and open as possible.*

# KNOWING MY NEEDS

I like to think of my needs as falling into two broad categories. The survival kind, which includes food, water, shelter, and sleep; the things we can't live without. And then there's the thriving kind.

The thriving kind of needs are things like connection, play, appreciation, and touch, to name a few. Getting these needs met is born from a desire to explore with curiosity the things we all crave beyond the basics of survival.

Different relationships in our lives lend themselves more easily to satisfying different needs. When we have a number of different people in our lives we can call upon to meet our needs, the more each relationship has space to flourish.

Often our romantic relationships start out being a place we go for touch, appreciation, and acceptance. The irony is that over time, if we aren't careful, these relationships can also become the place where we don't receive any of those things.

Why is that? I think a lot of it has to do with putting too much pressure on our partners to meet our needs and having the relationship turn into a place of obligation instead of a playground of desire.

I grew up thinking that I needed to find one partner who could meet the vast majority of, if not all of, my needs. The fairytale "you complete me."

I remember being out on a walk with one of my girlfriends as we were sharing how much pressure it is for one person to think they have to be everything for me. Expecting one person in my life to be everything for me every day is a very tall order and one that leads to inevitable failure.

Can I really expect one person to be my friend, my love, my business partner, my coach, my girl time playmate? It's not possible—beyond what's anatomically obvious. Sorry boys, you will never be one of my girls.

This has been such a wonderful concept for me to grasp.

I have my friends I call when I am a mess and crying my eyes out. I have my OM partners that I call to receive touch without a thought of compensation. I have my boyfriend, the man I love, who provides me with incredible stability and in many ways an unconditional love I have never experienced before. I have groups I join to learn how to be a better writer and the classes I attend to learn how to country line dance.

Our needs can be met in so many ways, and it is not

possible to expect one person to meet them all. Some needs are met through time with others, some are met with times of solitude, and some are met through multiple people and environments.

## STEPPING OUTSIDE

When I told David I wanted to practice Orgasmic Meditation with other people because he didn't want to do it, I was initially flooded with guilt. By realizing I have needs for touch and receiving, and it is totally okay to not be dependent on one person to meet them, I was able to release the guilt. When the guilt faded, I was able to more easily commit to meeting those needs met outside of him.

When I let that realization sink in, it was painful and liberating. When I love someone, I don't want to think about not needing them, and I don't want to think that they wouldn't need me. But love doesn't flourish from necessity. It flourishes from desire and from feeling excited to have the other in my life because they add to what I already have in a beautiful way.

The best relationships, in my experience, are a complement to a life that is led with self-responsibility and the knowledge that I am responsible for my own happiness. I take that off your plate and make it mine.

There is a quote I love from Jim Rohn that says, "I'll take care of me for you, if you will take care of you for me." Time and time again these words ring so true. Two people, no matter how much they love each other, will never be the other. We are all individuals that go through life's ebbs and flows.

Staying together because you need each other is not the way. Staying together because you want each other and are tuned in to your needs and the ways you can get them met is a very good start.

## DIFFERENT PLACES AT THE SAME TIME

Sometimes it aligns perfectly that we want the same things at the same time, and sometimes that couldn't be further from the truth.

It doesn't make either one of us wrong, but it does mean that we can't try to make the other happier than ourselves. It also doesn't mean that we give up our desires *or* our love.

It means that we recognize that, in this moment, we have different wants that are important to us and we trust that our love is deeper than the aspirations and transitions that we go through. We make a choice, a conscious one, to love each other through it all.

The more I give myself permission to acknowledge and feel the truth of the fact that I need more than one person in my life to meet all my needs, the more I feel connected with my partner and fulfilled by our relationship.

The pressure is off—and he can feel it. I no longer expect him to be my best friend; my passionate, kinky, and romantic lover; my teacher; my adventure partner; my coffee date; my stable provider; and my wild fling. He certainly can be all those things at one time or another, but I no longer expect him to be my everything *all the time.*

I trust that if I need to play and he isn't up for it, it's my responsibility to find play elsewhere instead of forcing it on him. Of course, it's a different story if I have a need that I truly want met with my romantic partner and it isn't happening enough for me to feel good about the relationship, but to expect my partner to meet all my needs will only lead to unnecessary heartache.

Stay tuned for the section on the Five Stages of Desire as I share an impactful journey I had in getting needs met outside of David.

*Take a look at the list of needs below and jot down on a piece of paper the ones you feel you could use more of in your life. If there are a number of them, that's okay. That is great awareness.*

*Once you have done that, choose one that you will focus on first.*

*Write down the people in your life you could reach out to for support to get this need met. Put a date and time on the calendar, whether it be with yourself or with another, to get this need met.*

*As you take the action, notice the ways it nourishes you, energizes you, and shifts how you feel in your body. If it has an impact on you in a way that makes you feel more alive, make a note of this somewhere and continue to prioritize this need.*

NEEDS:

- Connection
- Appreciation
- Acceptance
- Peace
- Play
- Clarity
- Purpose
- Honesty
- Autonomy
- Control
- Interdependence
- Trust
- Safety
- Expression
- Support
- Celebration
- Health
- Touch
- Movement
- Empathy

# BE HONEST

I have a love/hate relationship with honesty. It's life-changing and liberating when exercised, but getting there can be challenging. Sometimes it doesn't have to be as hard as we make it though. Sometimes it's just a matter of refining what we want or speaking our desires sooner rather than later.

## THE DRIVE HOME

We were driving back from my birthday weekend getaway, and I felt myself getting irritable with a sense of urgency to open my mouth and list off all my reasons for discontent. I felt like I had told David one too many times what I wanted from him. I started to go off about what had upset me from the weekend. I seemed to be finding several things to complain about until I remembered to ask myself, "What's the thing I am *really* upset about?"

Wait, did I ask myself? Or did he ask me? I forget. I might have been a little caught up in my emotions.

The thing about being honest when sharing desires and needs when I'm not practiced at it is that it can come out like water surging out of a fire hydrant. Full force, all over the place and messy.

Sometimes this is what needs to happen when you don't have a practice of being honest or sharing what's on your mind. For a long time, I was not experienced in being honest at all about my feelings or when something was bothering me. I had to let it be sloppy and unrefined until I got better at it. Heck, I'm still getting better at it.

Over time, I've learned some tricks to make it all a smoother process. One of those is to share a desire sooner rather than later so that it doesn't build enough internal pressure to make me want to blow. Another tip is that if you feel like the person hears you but isn't "getting it," perhaps you haven't been specific enough.

## THE LIGHTBULB

On this birthday excursion, the one I referred to above, I had asked for slow sex multiple times, and I didn't feel like he had given me what I wanted. He seemed excited about his plan for it, but when it happened, I was wondering in my head what he could have been thinking. Certainly not my version of slow.

"Did he even listen to me when I spoke to him?" I doubted in my head.

So, I started a fight about something else. Other things were irritating me too. So, we got into it and eventually, after far too much unnecessary drama, I circled back to the question that was most perplexing for me.

The conversation went something like this:

Me: "I have been asking you for slow sex, and you haven't given it to me. What the hell?!"

David: "I have been giving you slow sex! I was really happy with myself last night. I couldn't have fucked you any slower than I did. I mean at some moments, I was barely moving my cock inside of you."

Me: "Oooooooooh, shit." (*Exhale.*)

David: "Yeah, that's what you said. You said you wanted slow sex, so I've been fucking you slower more regularly, you seemed to like it. Didn't you see how I did it last night?"

Me: "Wow. Okay, yes, that felt good *and* that totally isn't what I meant. I was asking for you to touch and kiss my whole body. Like, I want you to get to my pussy last...and only after you have kissed and touched my arms, torso, legs, and feet."

Him: "Well then why didn't you just ask for that?"

Let me tell you, this was a massive lesson in realizing that no two people think alike and that if I want something, I had better be willing to be specific about it, and or to have the awareness to help the person I am with refine how they are doing something if I think it can be done better for me.

What slowed me down was when he reassured me and reminded me how often he listens to me and responds to me when I give him a specific request. He listens more than I give him credit for, and he wants to please me, so it's my responsibility to be clear.

## THE AFTERMATH

About a week later, we were sitting on the sofa watching the Dodgers game and David looked over at me. "Baby, I think we need to get a sensual massage together, you know, the kind where they give you a happy ending."

I looked back over at him and smiled. I have grown to get excited when he has a new idea about trying something together. I told him to go ahead, look it up, and see what he could find. He stumbled upon Tantric Sensual Massage.

I told him that I was open to it. He loves the idea of getting a massage and having someone give him a hand job at the end, and I love touch, period. The question crossed my mind, "Is that even legal to get happy endings at the end of a massage?" My concern passed quickly as it felt irrelevant to this inspired investigation. I wanted to see where he was going with this.

As we sat there watching the Dodgers game, I knew he was up to something. I had a suspicion it was something good, so I kept my mouth shut as he scrolled through his phone. As the game ended, he looked over at me and said, "Baby, I need you in our bedroom." We've learned to lovingly call our bedroom, "Pookie's workshop." He knows my sexual curiosity and often makes an effort to have something fun to explore.

That night was a treat that left me in tears. As I suspected, he had looked up Tantric Massage, and he gave me a magical gift of incredible attention and connection. He made it all about me and encouraged me to focus on my breath, receive, and feel it all.

Focusing on my breath during sex was something new to me, and as I did it, it amplified everything. Focusing on my breath made everything feel more...well, sensational. He touched my body, giving me my version of slow, not his. It was beautiful.

He brought over something called a body wand, which has a long cylindrical handle with a wide and thick top, probably about the width of a softball, with a flat, ridged firm surface. At first glance, I caught myself getting nervous and filled with anticipation wondering what the heck this thing was and how he was going use it.

I exhaled as he reminded me to breathe and let in the sensation. He placed it against the surface of my pussy and turned it on so I could feel the vibrations, asking me to let him know where it felt best as he played with different directions and locations.

He propped me up with pillows so I could let my body completely relax into the bed and began to ease his cock into my pussy, slowly. I could feel my pussy swollen from all the pleasure and relaxation. As he kissed my back and slid all the way in, I could feel my whole body exhaling and letting go of tension with each exhale.

## THE REWARD

Although there are moments of being honest that end up feeling great, some are messy. We have disagreements and misunderstandings, but there is no way around it. The more we see it as part of the territory, the less we take things personally and the more we share and refine together.

Practice being honest and sharing what you want. Try it in suggestions, try it in specific instructions. Be playful. Be serious. Learn with as much curiosity and open-mindedness as you can about yourself, your partners, and those around you. We all hear things differently and it can take a few minutes, or even years, to refine communication.

SPARK

*Think back to a time where you felt like you received partially what you wanted, but not the full deal. How could it have been even better? What could you have asked for to let yourself more fully receive?*

*Practice asking for it. Try asking the person directly. If that feels too scary, try role playing with a friend or coach. You can even brainstorm a potential script and practice asking in the mirror to see how it feels.*

# PART III
# THE FIVE STAGES OF DESIRE

# THE BASICS

When following a desire, there are five basic steps I like to follow, especially when the desire feels like a big one. When I follow these steps, I am able to more gracefully move from desire to desire and give myself permission to want more.

These steps, which I will break down in more detail as you read on, include:

1. Acknowledging your desire
2. Determining boundaries that feel good and safe to live out your desire
3. Taking action on the desire
4. Reviewing your thought process
5. Releasing what doesn't serve you

As I share this desire cycle, I will take you through my experience of listening to and acting on my desires. Without following these five steps, I would have stopped letting bigger desires in. I would have had an experience of fulfilling a desire and then found a way to cut myself off from wanting more, whether it be from guilt and shame or feeling like I don't deserve it.

The blessing and the curse is that the fastest way to see what is blocking me from living with more desire is to take action on a desire. I love these steps because they have allowed me to see that it's inevitable to have my fears, critical voices and reservations come up, but I can learn to work with them and get to know them instead of trying to pretend they don't exist or fighting them.

# ACKNOWLEDGE IT

Remember when I shared how my coach told me that the most painful secrets are the ones we keep from ourselves? Have you ever had the feeling that you aren't being fully honest with yourself about what you want?

As you've seen from getting to know me in this book, it took me a while to start asking myself what I wanted. Acknowledging what you want is one of the greatest gifts you can give to yourself.

There are a couple big reasons why it's such a gift:

The first gift is that when we acknowledge a desire, it puts us in touch with how bad we want it. If you start to do a regular practice of writing down your desires, you'll notice that some come up once that you'll rarely see again, while others will come up every time and pull at you harder and harder until you listen.

The second gift is that honesty with ourselves about what

we want leads us to become more aware of the discomfort we feel by not having it. When that discomfort increases, it will drive us to move in the direction of finding out what is preventing us from having what we want.

There is no rush when you are in this place, and I believe strongly that you'll do it when you are ready, but at least do yourself the favor of acknowledging what you want.

Once you've done that, I'd recommend taking it a step further. Tell someone you know. A friend, your significant other, someone who will hold your desire with kindness, encouragement, and curiosity. Perhaps this person can even help you bring your desire to life as well.

The thing about sharing a desire is that it's a mini action on stepping into that desire. It allows you to move a bit closer and see how it feels to put your desire out there in the world.

In my experience, sometimes sharing the desire is enough that it dissolves and no longer carries as much significance or weight. I simply don't want it anymore. Other times, when I share a desire, I realize how giddy it makes me feel and fills me with excitement to bring it to life.

## THE VICTORY

I had a curious experience one day when I shared lunch with an attractive, intriguing man during a lunch break at one of the courses I was participating in. I had a boyfriend, but I was enjoying this new man's company; the conversation, the playfulness, it was nice and warm, and I felt full of appreciation for the experience.

During the afternoon lectures, I kept having the thought, "I want to tell him that I appreciated talking to him and that I am attracted to him." It wasn't like I wanted to be with him or break up with my boyfriend, I just felt compelled to tell him that I found him and our connection to be fun, inviting and inspiring.

As the end of the day approached, I was committed to finding him and telling him about the attraction I felt. I could feel my heart beating in my chest as I tracked him down and knew that he was within a few steps of me. Before I could talk myself out of it, I approached him and opened my mouth, "I just wanted to say I felt an attraction to you today. I really enjoyed our conversation and sharing lunch together." He smiled and shared that he felt the same.

It was strange. Once I said it, and he acknowledged it, we both looked at each other and the conversation felt complete. We hugged with gratitude and went our separate ways. It was a perfect example, the most clear and simple one I have, of having a desire, sharing it, and having that be enough.

I had all this fear that if I told him I was attracted to him, it would snowball into me cheating on my boyfriend, or that I would be flooded with guilt, or that he would laugh at me as I stumbled through telling him I found him to be attractive. "Who does that?" I doubted myself. Who goes up to someone and just says, "I find you attractive," with no agenda? Yet I tried it, and it felt really good.

Being honest with yourself and someone else about your desires is so massively important. Sometimes it comes with ease, and sometimes it feels like a tremendous struggle. I remember a time very clearly when David and I shared a desire together. It was extremely difficult and left us both feeling like we might be on the verge of a breakup.


## THE STRUGGLE

We were in the parking lot at the grocery store and David told me he wanted us to have the freedom to have sex with other people. I could barely hear the words coming out of his mouth, I wanted to shut this whole conversation down. My body immediately became stiff and my mind foggy and unresponsive, and the only words coming out of my mouth were accusatory and defensive.

He told me it was bothering him that we weren't having sex with other people, and I was *angry* with him. *Very angry,* hurt, and my brain continued to fog up with confusion.

How dare he tell me this? *What was wrong with him?*

I could not gain my composure. I was distraught, like Moaning Myrtle in the Hogwarts bathroom.

He said, "Okay, we are going to head back home." We drove home empty-handed, as we never actually did the shopping we intended to because I just wanted to flee the situation. When we arrived home, we stepped into the bedroom. I was frigid with crossed arms, crossed legs, a scrunched-up face and clenched jaw. I knew that a part of me wanted the same thing, but it was a faint whisper and one that scared the shit out of me.

The idea of even having the freedom to have sex with other people felt liberating, but there was so much fear around what it would mean for us. I loved him, and people who love each other don't have sex with other people...right?!

But this is the thing about desire when it's true. It mounts, and continues to mount...one way or another, until its strength exceeds that of the fear.

There are many factors that go into acknowledging desire, one of which is whether or not I am considering my desire to be acceptable enough. If I consider that what I want is somehow "inappropriate," I am going to be more likely to want to hide it.

The question comes to mind: What will it mean about me if I admit that desire?

Have you ever acted revolted when someone shared a desire with you, but a part of you actually felt excited on the inside about the possibility? Maybe sensations arose within your body so quickly and drastically that you didn't know if you could handle it? When this happens to me, it is often because I have an emotional trigger around that desire and I'd do better to slow down and pay attention rather than judge and respond quickly.

At one time or another, I have made all my desires mean something about me: my desire to masturbate made me weird and shameful, my desire to have sex with another woman meant that I was a lesbian and sexually confused, my desire to have sex with a man that was not my boyfriend made me a cheating slut.

We all make our desires mean all kinds of things about us,

and we'll get further into what to do about this later on in the book. In the meantime, one of my favorite things to do when a desire surfaces is to have a small flip-style notebook and write down what I hear in my head when a desire arises.

SPARK

*Think of something you want that feels out of your comfort zone; it might even be something you consider yourself "wrong" for wanting.*

*Once you have that desire in your head, fill in the blanks with the prompt below:*

*My desire for _____ means that I am _____.*

*Feel free to jot down any and everything that comes up without censor.*

*In this exercise, all you are doing is being an observer. Be as curious as you can with yourself.*

*Were you surprised by what came up? Did this provide you with any new insight? Or are you hearing a similar voice that you've perhaps heard for years?*

We were standing in the bathroom when David looked at me with soft eyes and said, "You want to have sex with him don't you?" My cheeks turned red as I looked down to break eye contact with him. He was inquiring about my desire to be with a friend of mine who I had indeed been wanting to have sex with. Not because I wanted to leave David, but because I was looking for something specific that I hadn't been getting with him.

I couldn't find any words as I scrambled, trying to determine whether or not to come out with the truth or make up some bullshit lie.

I caved and told him the truth. A slower, more connected sex was what I had been craving. I wanted it with David, but he admittedly wasn't in a place where he wanted to give it to me. But I still wanted it, and I knew where I could get it.

It felt terrifying and liberating to admit that I did want to have sex with John, so much so that I hadn't trusted myself to hang out with him lately. We were OM partners that had developed a friendship in the process. It was the first time since being with David that I was truly honest with myself about wanting to have sex with a man who wasn't him.

I spent so much of our relationship denying that I felt any attraction to anyone else. I didn't want to admit that I had any interest in others, no matter how small. I had prided myself on being loyal and dedicated. I told myself that loyal and dedicated people don't have attractions to multiple people.

When David and I first got together, my ex-husband had been out of the house for three months. I hadn't had sex with anyone else but him for the past seven years, and I felt like I was on the verge of a sexual revolution. David told me to take my time, to have sex with other people. He had the sense that it would be good for me to have experiences with multiple partners before I settled into a relationship. I wouldn't do it.

Over a year later when we found ourselves in the bathroom having this conversation, I did *not* feel comfortable, and I had an "oh fuck" moment. *Maybe I should have listened to him about being with other people? Is it too late?*

David's mother had passed away less than six months ago, and I had just moved into his childhood home with him. We were both adjusting. My response was to energize and replenish through sex, playfulness, and connection. He was in a place of retreat and healing and did not share my desire for lots of slow connected sex at that time.

I took a deep breath as I admitted: "Yes, I have been thinking about having sex with John, and I would like to do it."

He already knew it. He's an amazing reflection for me of what I am holding back. He puts it in my face so I can't avoid it, but he does it in a very loving and patient way. Oh, it's confronting as hell. But it doesn't feel malicious, and it provokes me to feel alive and full of sensation.

He was not angry with me. He was willing to have a

conversation, and I was given the opportunity to own my desire. There was no shame or guilt thrown at me. We both know that living our relationship as though we are each other's possessions will only lead to heartache in the end anyway.

It can be hard at times to feel deeply in love with someone and to navigate sexual desires. Especially when they aren't always exclusively with my partner.

## HIS DESIRE

When David first told me he wanted to be able to have sex with other women, I flipped out. I made it mean that he didn't love me, that we were destined to break up, that he didn't think I was pretty, and that the list of women he saw as more beautiful than me was ever-increasing and pushing me off the map.

What I've learned to be true is that when my partner tells me his desires, he is being brave. He believes in our relationship and wants us to be together, or connected in some capacity, because he is willing to tell me what is neither easy nor quick. Listening to desire requires a heavy amount of surrender and an ability to accept what is. To hear it with an open ear and heart without jumping to conclusions.

I convinced myself, quite easily I might add, that David was wrong, or I defaulted to being upset with him many times for him wanting to have sex with another woman, and there I was with these same desires of my own.

Until this time, I never would have considered in a million years that I could have desire for someone beyond my man. The question of loyalty, as I shared, was present for me in this process and as the thought of sex with others came up for me, I began to ask myself: Can I have sex with other people and still be considered loyal? Oh boy, did this question fuck me up. For a long while, the only logical answer seemed to be, "No."

I'm grateful we acknowledged our desires because it opened me up to the truth that, yes, I can be loyal *and* explore my desire, even if it involves venturing outside of my relationship. After we acknowledged that, we started on a path of figuring out what was next. Because this was all new, I started to investigate and figure out what I would need for boundaries to move forward and follow through.

# SPARK

*Similar to what you did at the beginning of this book, pull out your journal, set out a timer for five minutes and begin with the sentence starter, "I want **to**..." and finish the sentence. Keep starting with these words, "I want **to**..." and finish the sentence until your timer goes off.*

*If you feel willing and ready (and even if it makes you a little squirmy and nervous), make the choice to share this list with someone. Perhaps it's with someone who can just listen and hold space for you, or maybe it's someone who can help you bring the desire to life.*

*It can be sexual or non-sexual; it can be anything you want. Let it be completely uncensored. You could even flush it down the toilet or burn it if you feel embarrassed, shy, or don't want anyone else to see it. Give yourself the gift of getting it down. This isn't a moment to worry about the future. It's a moment to be true to yourself about what you want.*

# SET BOUNDARIES

Once you have acknowledged the desire, it's time to discuss and determine boundaries. Just like with acknowledging the desire, it's helpful to explore this both internally and externally.

I find it helpful to explore boundaries and come to agreements for a couple of reasons. Acting on a desire involves newness, feeling butterflies, and change. When we can create a container or a kind of sacred space to explore, it offers a greater sense of safety to trying something new.

Remember, as much as we love adventure, we are also creatures that crave safety. The more we find a place for both of those needs to co-exist, the better the result.

When I initially started masturbating, I decided that I was going to set a ten-minute timer to give myself a massage and do the best I could to stay present as I got closer to my pussy. It was helpful for me to have a time frame I would allot and when the timer went off, I could stop. It took the pressure off. I shared about the first time earlier in the book, and as I continued it got easier. Knowing I had a start and end time helped me get started.

My Orgasmic Meditation practice also showed me the power of boundaries and a space to completely let go and receive. I knew exactly what I was getting into, and my only job was to relax into it in the safety of the container that was created.

Setting more than just time boundaries are important when we are exploring desires, especially sexual ones outside of our partners. I don't believe in doing something willy-nilly and disregarding the feelings of those I love, but I also know that it's not okay to deny myself something just because I am meeting resistance.

Taking the time to research and think about boundaries, current levels of willingness, and safety is crucial in helping to reduce feeling frantic and scared.

## THE RESEARCH

After my confession to David in the bathroom, I went through a researching period where everything became more real. I started to look up why I was pulled to an open relationship and found questions I could ask myself to consider all the options.

One of those important questions was: *Why* do you want to do it?

My research was encouraging me to be clear about what I was not getting in my relationship that I would want to get from an experience outside of it.

When I journaled, I knew what I wanted. I wanted to be looked at with love. I wanted to be hugged knowing I had his full attention. I wanted us to kiss when we had sex, and I wanted us to take our time and feel connection together, and that wasn't happening like I wanted it to.

I decided to muster up the courage to talk to him about this. One day when he came home, I sat down with him and explained what I was looking for. I shared that I wanted a slower, more connected sex and that I was craving more touch and eye contact.

He listened and let me know that he had to be honest, he didn't know if and when he would ever get back to a place of wanting to connect like that. He was devastated by the loss of his mother and had admittedly shut down. I couldn't speed up his healing process, especially not by trying to force it.

He lovingly let me know that he wasn't willing to go there with me right now and that he respected if I wanted to seek that connection outside of us. So, it became clear. I knew I had to do it. And I knew who I wanted to do it with.

It would be John. I knew he would slow down for me, I could ask him for what I wanted, and I knew from our friendship that he would give me the attention and connection I requested. He had a touch in our OM practice that filled me with anticipation and desire, and I often left our practice feeling alive, excited and full of gratitude. Our OMs often felt like they had a healing and alchemical aspect to them.

This became a bit of a rub for David. He admittedly

struggled with the person I wanted to live out this desire with. He requested that I have sex with someone that I didn't feel as strong a connection with.

I reminded him slow connection was the whole point of the experience for me.

For David, his desire around sex with other women was more for fun and variety. He was struggling to see that I wanted more connection and had a realistic fear of what if it became sex *and more*? Which, when he reminded me to turn the tables and put myself in his shoes, I got it.

David asked me to consider a friend of his, one he felt comfortable with and that he knew was in a committed relationship where the risk was lower. I considered giving myself only half of my desire by having the opportunity to have sex with someone new that may or may not be open to my requests and that I didn't have the same level of connection with.

I remember mulling it over with a friend while we went for an evening stroll. As she heard me talk about my options, she looked at me very plainly and with confidence as she reflected back to me that I already knew what I wanted, and it didn't make sense to try to settle on this one.

The reality was that David told me he wasn't willing to go there with me. If I was confident I wanted and could have a triple fudge sundae, why would I only give myself a single scoop of vanilla? I mean...really now. It just didn't seem worth it. And if I was going to take the risk, why not just go all out with it?

DISCUSSING TERMS

When I finally came to terms with this desire, and we agreed it would be John, David and I got into a conversation to discuss the boundaries we would need to make sure we both felt comfortable.

He made three requests...well, actually four.

"There will be no cuming in your mouth," he declared. My mouth was reserved for his cum...which I was definitely comfortable with. No anal sex. My ass was his, which I also felt fine with. And no sleepovers. I would come home afterwards. This worked perfectly for me, as I knew that I didn't want to stay over.

...and finally, if afterwards there was a thought that I would want more with John than just occasional sex and a friendship, that we discuss it and I would consider no longer having the friendship with John.

The final request was the hardest on many levels. I enjoyed this friendship, wanted to maintain it in some way after having sex, and I wasn't psychic. I mean, I felt strongly that it was about sex and connection and nothing more. But I didn't know for sure.

What if I went through with it and felt like there was something else behind it? How would I navigate that?

I made peace with the fact that this was one of those times where I had a choice, but didn't really, because the desire was so strong. I knew that if I didn't follow through with this desire that I would have regrets.

I had some practice with expressing desires and having

them fade once I shared them. This wasn't one of those times. It felt like the longer I went without it, the more I wanted it. I very much loved my boyfriend, but I also had a desire to have sex with other people, and it wasn't going away.

I agreed to the terms we discussed as well as the commitment to use condoms, which felt like a given, but we took a moment to clarify. Negotiations were complete, and I was following through with my desire. I called John to tell him where we were at with boundaries and he agreed to it all.

## LOGISTICS & TIMING

It was now a question of logistics. David was going away for a weekend to a bachelor party and he liked the idea of me doing it while he was away. In hindsight, I don't know if that was best, but I'll come back to that. We made the decision, and I connected with John. I would go to his place the Saturday that David was away, and we would have sex. A sex appointment, you could call it.

My choice to explore having sex with someone outside of my committed relationship was one that took months to sink in. It tapped into a few major taboos for me around what is and isn't okay in committed relationships. Some desires, the ones that don't test my belief systems so much, are easier to jump into, but this was a more challenging one for me.

I gave myself permission in this process with David to move slower and sink it all in because it was so new. For some desires, this phase of setting boundaries and parameters might happen in your mind in the matter of a few seconds, but other times it might require a longer period of journaling, reflecting, or conversation.

Relationships are complex, and I will admit to having the tendency to be a runner. If things aren't great in a given moment, I tend to want to run and escape instead of facing it and breaking it down. It's a practice that gets better with practice, and I have to continually remind myself of that.

It was tremendously challenging and rewarding for me to go through the process of knowing I wanted more than what I was currently getting from my relationship but also being willing to stay in the discomfort and anticipation of wanting more and not knowing completely how it would all come to life.

## BOUNDARIES ARE THERE FOR A REASON

Boundaries are so valuable. I can't stress enough that if you set a boundary with someone, and you value the relationship, respect it. Maintain the integrity of what you have agreed upon. You can set boundaries and redefine them as you go, but especially if you are new to something —stick to it!

Boundaries help us define our comfort limits and the zone we'd like to stay in to preserve a certain level of safety. Although your comfort levels will likely grow and surpass where you are now, if you do it too fast or with too much force, a relationship can be lost, or you can slow your longer-term progress.

If someone tells you a boundary, listen to them. If

someone tells you they are doing the best they can, believe them. If your partner tells you that they aren't ready for you to be having sex with someone else even though you want to, believe them.

If it's important for you and you want to maintain the relationship, try discussing smaller steps to lead up to the bigger desire.

I am a fan of following desires with transparency for all involved. Even though up front it's harder, it feels cleaner and more satisfying when it's all said and done.

## THE WRAP UP ON BOUNDARIES

A key to remember with boundaries is to do the research and have the conversations you need to in order to make sure that you (and your partner, if relevant) feel safe in moving forward on a given desire.

These boundaries can include time frames, locations, safety checks, and anything else you need in order to be a *full yes* to following through on any given desire. When I say *full yes*, I mean you experience a "Hell yeah baby!" or an "I'm so ready," or even a "My stomach is full of butterflies, but let's do this!" The nerves of a new experience may, and probably will, be present, but the trust that you want this (whatever it is) is clear and unwavering within you.

If you are going to be negotiating boundaries with your partner, trust them when they tell you their boundaries. Ask them questions, be curious, and also respect their no's. I've learned with my partner that a "no" can even disguise itself as a maybe. If you or your partner have any doubt, my recommendation would be to talk through it and be curious about why. Does something else have to be explored before you can both feel comfortable?

If you are reading this chapter with a desire in mind that you would like to act on and you are not sure how this whole boundaries thing ties in, ask yourself: Am I ready to take action on my desire? Is there anyone else in my life that would be affected by me taking action that I may want to discuss boundaries with? (Think: How would I feel if I were in their shoes?)

If you feel like you (or they) are not ready, here are some questions you can ask: What would need to happen for me to be a *full yes* to taking action on this desire? What is a smaller step I can take that feels better for me? What do I need physically or emotionally to feel ready, willing, and excited about this? You can also ask these same questions to the person that would be affected by the decision to get a feel for where they are at.

# SPARK

*Take a look at a recent desire list you wrote and ask yourself: What is one desire I would like to explore further? What boundaries do I need to feel comfortable bringing this desire to life?*

*I recommend doing this as a journaling exercise where you set a 5-10 minute timer and write down whatever comes up in response.*

*In line with the text above, some things to journal about are:*

- *What do I need to feel physically and emotionally safe?*
- *Who will be impacted by this decision and how would I feel if I put myself in their shoes?*
- *Are there any smaller steps I can take that feel exciting and fun to me that would lead me closer to living out this desire?*

*See what comes up and practice establishing boundaries with yourself and others.*

# TAKE ACTION

The third step is to take action. The beauty of action, no matter how big or small, is that it brings three important things. One of those things is clarity. When I am scared, I remind myself action is what gives me hints as to whether or not I want more of something.

Two, taking action shows you where you still have fear or are holding yourself back. I remind myself often that one of the fastest ways to see what is in the way of going after what I want is to take a step towards it. The trick is not to take any feedback as the end-all-be-all, but to know that it's all information to help clear the path to a bigger, bolder, and more fabulous life filled with not just desire, but fulfilled desires.

The third thing you get is an opportunity to be as present as possible to all the sensations and gifts that come from being brave enough to take action on what you want. This might be the trickiest of them all for the self-improvement driven people out there like myself that are continually striving to be better. The reason I say this, for me, is because wanting to always be better can leave me stuck in my head, feeling like I can't get out. There is a time to reflect, and in the heat of action is not one of them.

## INEVITABLE NEW ROADS

One of the reasons I have a love/hate relationship with my desire at times is because when I listen to it, it opens up new roads, forks, and terrain to navigate. This can be super exciting and equally nerve-wracking.

What is following this desire going to do for me? And my relationships?

What desires will stem from taking action on this one?

Many times, these questions were almost enough to keep me in paralysis and not able to move forward. I heard a motivational speaker say once, "When you can't walk, crawl." This is so true. Resistance will arise when you go for what you want. Let it be there, give it a voice, negotiate with the resistance if need be, and keep going.

Sometimes I try to trick or convince myself into believing that I can know what's next without taking action. The hamster wheel in my mind works on overdrive to find the answers until I say to myself, "Slow it down, woman. You have to live this one to know what is next."

Below are some beautiful words by Rainer Maria Rilke that really lay out how action is *the way* to get answers to our questions.

*"Be patient toward all that is unsolved in your heart and try to love the questions themselves, like locked rooms and*

*like books that are now written in a very foreign tongue.
Do not now seek the answers, which cannot be given you
because you would not be able to live them. And the point
is, to live everything. Live the questions now. Perhaps you
will then gradually, without noticing it, live along some
distant day into the answer."*

And that is exactly what I did.

## THE ARRIVAL

I drove to my friend John's, where I had gone many times
before to OM and hang out with specific boundaries in
mind. We would chat, OM, share our reflections, and that
would be it.

But today it was different. I was going to my sex
appointment.

Do I dress differently? Do I prepare in a way that I
haven't before? I made a few decisions very consciously;
one of them was that I would not wear any lingerie that
David had given me. It somehow felt safer and cleaner
emotionally to have this be fully my experience by not
bringing anything intimate into it that David had
given me.

We were meant to meet at 7pm. I'm usually quite
punctual, but I found a way to delay my arrival until
closer to 8pm as I was going back and forth in my head
about whether or not I was going to follow through
with this.

When I finally made my way to his address, I came to the
door shyly and awkwardly saying, "Hi," in a casual yet

tight red dress. I decided on wearing a matching forest green lace bra and pantie set underneath that I had bought for myself months prior. David didn't care for it, but it made me feel sexy, so it felt like the perfect lingerie choice.

We made our way to his bedroom and started talking a bit. All kinds of doubts and questions came into my mind: Do I sit or stand? How do I rest my hands? How long do we have small talk before we just cut to the chase and do this?

As we were lying there talking, I couldn't help but think, "What the fuck am I doing? If you do this, you can't go back!"

He let a hand rest on my body to ground me and drop me a bit further out of my head. A more intimate touch was initiated with a kiss on the lips, and almost immediately the thought popped into my head, "Shit, your lips aren't like David's. David kisses me differently."

I wasn't sure that I was going to be able to go through with this. I think we both left the room at least twice to go to the restroom within a 45-minute time frame. Close to an hour passed of talking and false starts before he finally stated calmly and clearly, "Jaclyn, we are not going to go through with this unless you can live in this moment...like we have no past or future. The only way you are going to do this is if you live in the present right now."

It hit me. That's what I came for—presence, full attention, and connection. I had to find the place where I could let the doubts and worry dissolve about what was to come. It was time to drop all the attention out of my head and into my body, to feel.

David's voice popped into my head too, "Babe, if you are going to do this, for real, enjoy it."

We decided to go through with it. Well, scratch that. He was already ready. I made the decision that I was ready... or as ready as I was ever going to be.

As we began to kiss, he whispered a request, "Kiss me how you'd like me to lick your pussy." Oh my goodness, I don't know if it sounds as hot to you reading it, but it made me melt like butter into the bed to hear those words. He was asking me to tell him what I wanted with a kiss. My body was so excited at the invitation to share what it wanted without a need for words that my back arched up, and I could feel my toes curling with anticipation.

I lifted my head so that my lips could meet his lips and gave him a soft, smooth kiss that lingered with a slight bite at the end. That kiss set the tone for our sex that night.

We made out for a few minutes and I was stripped down to my bra and panties. He found his way down to my pussy by gliding his hands down my torso and over my legs. His touch was soft and slow. With each touch, I felt myself exhaling and relaxing more into it.

I recognize I'm a slow melt at times. I can become closed off and frigid, faster and more than I'd like to admit. The melting process sometimes takes me longer than I desire, but touch does it.

Touch can transport me out of the loops of my mind to a place where my body rules if I let it. To a place where feeling good matters, where all of my attention is actually on what is happening in that very moment.

It's a place where everything feels possible and nothing really fucking matters. Or, at the very least, everything that does matter is right in front of me and it's all working out.

As he reached for my panties to pull them down, I lifted my butt and started to help him. He asked me to stop and let him do it. "Oh my goodness, for real," I smiled inside. "Now *this* is receiving."

He asked me to just relax and take it in. He took his time and made it all about me, finding his own joy in the experience. In moments like these, the experience itself feels like a sanctuary where relief, bliss, and possibility are all present.

He went down on me as I lost track of time, letting myself enjoy and sink deeper into my body with every smooth wet lick of his tongue. He eventually crawled his way up, positioning his body right over mine, and he hovered with the tip of his cock right at the entrance of my pussy and kissed my lips.

It was a crazy sensual and hot experience to feel him staying at the point where he was just barely inside of me. My whole body lay in anticipation as he held himself above me with his skin centimeters away from mine, creating a magnetic pull.

Our sex was slow and present. At times, as we lay in missionary position, he was barely moving as I could feel the inside of my vagina gently pulsing. We were in no rush, in fact, neither of us came. There were moments of bite that were passionate and heated, where he thrust deep and hard inside of me, and he brought with them anticipation and excitement for the unexpected changes of pace.

I got exactly what I came for. I could feel all the energy that was drained from me in my normal day-to-day start to replenish. The experience truly felt complete. I felt like I had full attention and connection. It was the slow I was looking for. It was safe, and I felt respected and cared for.

As we finished the night, he took a minute to lay on top of me and give me the full weight of his body. This is something I have come to cherish after sex. Although sex is awesome and life-giving, it can leave me feeling like I'm floating or in the clouds sometimes. A bit of grounding afterwards goes a long way.

As we sat up, he asked me to share one of my favorite moments from the night and he shared his. I remember sharing the moment where he was just about to enter inside of me and I could feel the anticipation with the pulsing of my pussy.

I left feeling expansive, light, satisfied, and full of gratitude.

When I got to my car, it didn't take long for me to start thinking about how I would share this experience with David. Do I feel bad that it felt good? Do I try to hide how good I felt about it? He told me I could go through with it, so he shouldn't be mad! But it was better than expected. How do I tell my partner I enjoyed having sex with someone else? Eek.

This action did what action does, it stimulated movement.

It got me fired up about what I wanted more of and showed me the parts of myself that resisted pleasure. It also brought about some intense and rewarding conversations for David and I, which I'll share as you read on.

## SUMMARY ON TAKING ACTION

When you take action, do your best to do just that, take action.

Breathe. Drop into your body. Notice the sensations you feel and do your best to stay with them. Let the time for analyzing and review come later, do the thing that you came to do and fully live in the moment.

If you are anything like me, you need a reminder to *enjoy it*.

You might feel awkward, and that's okay. If it's a new desire you are acting on, it's inevitable that it will feel awkward or a little strange.

# SPARK

What is something you desire sexually? What is one action step you can take towards making it a reality?

Is it treating yourself to an outfit that makes you feel sexy and wearing it out with a friend? Is it flirting with the guy at that checkout counter that you always thought was cute?

Take an action on something that makes you feel sexy or fills you with a feeling of butterflies and excitement.

Let it feel awkward and playful and silly and new.

# REVIEW

Taking action on this desire stirred up a lot from within. It brought up excitement for more, fear for what was next, and anticipation for what was to come for David and I.

In this chapter, we'll dive into the aftermath of my sexual encounter and the voices of gratitude, criticism, and fear that came up as a result of taking pleasurable action. I'll also share some critical voices that have come up on my road to pleasure that you might hear on your journey.

## RECONNECTING

When I left John's place, I called David in Las Vegas as we agreed on to let him know I went through with it and that I was safe and at home. We had a very brief conversation as he let me know that he was out with his friends and we would talk the next day. I thought to myself, "He must be mad at me; he is being cold and short."

I hung up the phone and could feel apprehension flowing through me. We decided before he left that I would pick him up at the airport the next day. Initially, I had anticipated his arrival with much excitement as I planned to dress sexy and have a super-hot and connected reunion.

The morning I was going to pick him up, I met up with one of my friends. We walked through a beautiful hilly path while I teetered back and forth from giddy school girl that had this super fun new sexual experience to nervous nelly about how I was going to put the experience into words for David.

When I left my friend and got into the car to head home before picking David up at the airport, he called me while sitting at the terminal waiting to board his flight. He asked me to tell him a bit more about my time with John. I asked him how much he wanted to know. He said, "Everything."

I said, "Are you sure? You told me initially that you didn't want to know details. Are you *really* sure you want to know?"

He said, "Yes."

So, I went on to tell him about the night, how it was just what I was looking for and how I got the attention and connection I went for. I shared what I liked and also slipped in there what I wanted more of with David that I had gotten from John.

I learned that my timing was not ideal on giving instructions on how he could be better. The key theme I was lacking in my replay was reassurance and gratitude.

I now know anytime I have sex with another person that is not my primary partner, and the plan is to stay with my primary partner, reassurance and gratitude needs to be part of the post-experience sharing. Just like I learned the sandwich approach with giving feedback in other areas of my life. I practice the same thing with sexual feedback.

I want to make sure I thank my partner for being supportive and loving through the process and express love and gratitude before I make any requests or indications of what they can do better.

At the time though, I was an amateur to this. I shared my experience with excitement, but then stumbled into fear that David and I might not have moments like that, and so I applied pressure that I wanted him to give me that same kind of attention, or else! (*Eeeeek.*) He felt hurt and I was frustrated. The thing we needed more than anything else, which was to touch and reconnect, was becoming less and less likely with each word we said.

As our compounding pride grew and we shut off from each other with each failed attempt at communication, I stepped away and called a friend crying. It's so frustrating to have those moments when I know all I want is to shut up and hug, but all we keep doing is clumsily making defensive comments that just freeze us off from one another. We both wanted to be right and to make our point, but all that was doing was increasing the rift between us.

She reminded me of the aliveness I was feeling from taking this action, which was great. What we were going through was all part of the process, but more than anything (as I suspected) we needed to shut up and hug, have some sex to reconnect, and stop rehashing our hurts.

That took a couple days to happen, but we got there eventually.

Words are great, but they reach their moment of diminishing returns. When they do, the best recommendation I can give is: *stop using them!* Touch instead. Then re-group and perhaps try a softer approach, one that starts with gratitude and acknowledgement.

## THE FEARS

One of my biggest fears was that David was going to change his mind, that his loving approval was going to turn into resentment and that this whole experience would be the start of the end for us.

I felt scared that his loving support would transform into an unkind retaliation. Mostly because if I was honest, I didn't know if I would be capable of what I was asking for: a loving reception and approval for getting my sexual desires met outside of him.

I knew my insecurity would kick in if he told me he enjoyed having sex with someone else. I would probably want to immediately know how I could do it better and what he learned. But that wasn't the way the tables were turned on this one, and he was able to listen to my experience and make it something we could grow from as a couple.

## THE OPENING

There were many unexpected blessings that occurred as a result of taking this action.

Although David told me he didn't have the attention or commitment in him to give me what I requested, when I committed with full transparency to get it elsewhere, something in him stepped up. It was an opportunity for him to check in on how much he loved me and wanted to share with me.

We had some pretty incredible conversations after that night where we shared our fears and what we wanted with one another. I am sure a significant factor in starting those conversations was the fact that I took a stand for what I wanted.

I remember sitting on top of David as he lay belly up on the bed opening up about how hard the last few months were. We were vulnerable and softened with our words and our hearts. I shared in a softer way what I was yearning for with him and that I missed feeling like my primary intimate partner was the person I could go to for warm, present, and connected love and affection.

It became a turning point for us in that way. It woke both of us up.

Sharing how I felt not only opened up the communication between David and I, it made us aware of the negative voices. That was a transformative night for us where we saw a different perspective of each other that we had never seen before.

I had a deeper understanding of his grieving process and

the ways he had been reaching out for connection with me in ways I wasn't seeing and he had the chance to understand my desires in a more receptive way. We put our shields down, let go of the thought that we needed to convince each other of anything, and really heard each other.

I shared my desires without attaching an ultimatum or judgment, which made it so much easier for him to hear. Who would have thought? *Huh.* Powerful stuff. "Keep that one in your memory bank, so you do that again," I thought to myself.

Taking this action created a tremendous amount of expansion inside of me. I saw how I could let more in and be true to my desire, and that, as a result, one way or another, I would get more of what I wanted.

Let me break down some key practices and questions that are super helpful when it comes to review of a new experience following action on a desire.

## FINDING THE GOOD

Before you start to dig deeper into the negativity that came up and how things could be better or should have been better: do a little happy dance, be proud of yourself, and recognize your bravery. You did something new that deserves acknowledgment. Be grateful to those that supported you or made it possible for you to follow through.

Celebrate yourself, the experience, and those that supported you.

Without time to stop and celebrate in review, it all becomes a pursuit of the next thing. I can tell you from experience that endless pursuit does not lead to more pleasure. This is a time to take a breath and a moment to bask in your greatness and willingness to explore a new part of yourself. Write it in a journal, call a friend, and dance around your house saying, "Woooo hooooo!"

When I left John's, I had a few moments of this. I had an intention to slow myself down even more to appreciate my actions and success. It felt really good to sink into the fact that I *did it!*

## ASK QUESTIONS

Some great questions to ask after action on a new desire are the following:

- What do I want more of as a result of following that desire?
- In what ways am I becoming critical of myself for taking action?
- What fears came up in the process of taking that action?
- What voices are coming up that feel like they are blocking me from letting in more desires? In what way am I resistant to more pleasure?

Let me share how these questions helped me to create an experience of more pleasure and bravery moving forward.

## I WANT MORE

After my night with John, I realized that I enjoyed feeling the full weight of his body on mine after sex. It was grounding and felt like it brought the experience full circle.

I was excited to tell David about this and do this with him as well.

I also loved that we didn't just rush up and out. We shared what we enjoyed about the experience and took a little time to speak and connect afterwards before we got dressed and carried on with the night.

I brought these practices back to David, and we make an effort to integrate them at least some of the time. As a result, it has improved our sex life, and I receive those moments of feeling heard and attended to that fill me up.

## GETTING TO KNOW THE RESISTANCE

Shortly after my new adventure, I felt like I needed support for some of the critical voices coming up. Although I was proud of myself, I was a bit shaken up from taking action that was out of character for me, and it was leading me to question myself and my expanded relationship with desire.

I joined a course to connect with other women on the path to increasing their ability to receive. Something the teacher shared one day was that as we grow, we often have similar blocks that come up at different levels of our path.

Each layer of growth brings with it the voices that remind us of how we are not good enough, not prepared enough, or not safe enough to keep moving forward. She told us that it makes sense to get to know these voices as soon as possible because they will be coming back.

For example, when I started to masturbate, I had similar critical voices. Also when I started dating without a finalized divorce and when I wanted to have sex with someone outside of my partner.

A couple of my loudest demons are the voices that tell me I am not good enough, I have to control the situation for it to be okay, and that I can't handle it. These voices came up again and again with the examples above. When it came to pleasure, it also came to my attention that I heard the voices of guilt running through me for experiencing more pleasure than I should have.

Let's talk about these critical voices.

## I'M NOT GOOD ENOUGH

This is a voice that has very much found its way into my thought process. The voice that I am not, and will never be, enough is one that can be tormenting, and it can literally take away every good feeling I have at a given moment.

Gosh, I remember a day when David told me that he liked a woman's outfit and he wanted to see me in it. I made that mean I was not enough. *Because he liked an outfit.* I made it mean that he thought she was prettier than I was, that I was less than her and would never meet up to his standard. My mind and my response to him was not a pretty sight.

No, no, no. Not anymore. I want to catch those voices *fast*. It's time to choose kindness with myself and remember that, yes, I am enough.

One of my favorite ways to respond to this voice is with a hand on my heart, reminding myself that, "I am enough," with the follow-up question, "Who is telling me I am not enough right now?" Is someone really telling me this right now or am I making an interaction mean something that it doesn't?

David sometimes jokes with me, saying he wishes he could be in my head to correct the ways I distort what he says. It's true, and I work to catch myself more each time. When I start to get critical, I remember to keep in mind: Is this truth or am I making all of this mean something it doesn't?

## I WANT CONTROL

If there is one thing I have loved more than anything over the years, it's been control. Control has been what has kept me safe in the hard times.

There was a time when I would spend less or no time with people that made me nervous. In fact, I would spend less time with people in general to decrease the chance of being uncomfortable. When I felt uncomfortably overweight and fearful, I would do this all the time. Instead of asking for support, I would cut myself off because at least then I knew what would be happening.

Giving up control in some ways requires more of me than controlling. Surrendering and relinquishing control always seems to mean feeling more and thinking less. Oh, but I love to think and rehash and rehash. Well, I did, and then I started to realize that it can actually be quite exhausting to live from this place of constantly thinking and managing what may or may not happen next.

I'm learning to focus on choice over control. When the fear arises, I can choose my breath instead of making attempts to control my environment. I can choose to say the vulnerable thing instead of saying something that will distance me more from my partner, and by that I mean say what is honest and true (not the thing that is manipulative or with an agenda).

Choice over control is one that requires practice, but it's worth it.


## GIVING UP CONTROL IN PRACTICE

I remember we were standing in line at IKEA after having a very emotional conversation about swinging. I confessed to wanting to try it and a bit reluctantly shared that I had been having thoughts about it for months.

David jokingly, yet not so jokingly said, "You mean you've been wanting ice cream all this time when I've been wanting it as well? Let's go get it."

As he said that and it sunk in, I could feel my body full of sensation and my pussy alive. Being honest about desires requires giving up control. Giving up control is often hard, not because it's physically laborious, but because it requires us to do something we aren't often taught how to do: *feel*.

It's a time to let the thoughts, judgments, opinions, and worry go and let something happen. It's when we feel the sensation of it all and to stay with it and keep coming back to it as much as possible.

When I give up control in some way and get nervous, I have to remind those fearful voices, "I love you. I hear you. Thanks for sharing. *And* right now, I'm having fun and feeling alive, so I'm going to keep doing this." I say these words to the voices as I might talk to my child (if I were to have one) in a grocery store who is screaming for my attention. I let the voices be heard because they are part of me, but I will choose to move forward regardless.

## YOU DESERVE TO BE PUNISHED

When I left John's apartment I remember saying to myself, you should be punished for the amount of pleasure you allowed yourself to have. I caught myself saying it, and I was like, "Hold up. Wow. Really? I have that thought?"

It's not surprising being that I was raised Catholic and seem to have freshly flowing guilt running through my veins as a default response to any behavior that is less than saintly and polite. I think many of us are familiar with the term "Catholic guilt." I don't acknowledge it to say that it's good or bad; I do it so those that were raised Catholic can check in when they start to feel guilty for no good reason.

So much of feeling bad isn't even our own "stuff." It's the

stuff of the societies, religions, history, and accumulated stereotypes we live in and around. Go deep enough inside of yourself to figure out if your desire feels right for *you*.

This time when I felt the guilt after my night with John, I thought, "Damn girl that is one strict internal policy to bring all that guilt on yourself."

When I look back, I see that I have often felt like pleasure was something I had to feel bad about and downplay. It was something bad girls went after or people that didn't have focus or goals.

With these more recent dives into pleasure, it wasn't feeling true anymore. It didn't have the same hold on me as it used to when I realized those thoughts weren't really mine to begin with.

As you may have heard, creating awareness around our thoughts is huge. Once we have awareness, we can do something about it. Take a look at the spark below and see if you resonate with any of the same critical voices that have come up for me over the years.

SPARK

*Start to learn your critical voices.*

*Here are some of the critical and restricting voices I have heard on my journey of exploring sexual desire (some from above, and some added):*

- *I can't have any sex because I might get an STD*
- *Someone will know I had this sexual experience and they won't like me or approve of me anymore*
- *Good girls don't... Bad girls do...and you were a bad girl*
- *You will be punished for this*
- *I have to control everything moving forward*
- *Something bad is going to happen now*
- *I can't handle it*
- *Having the sex I want will makes me a slut*
- *That's dirty or doing that would make me a dirty person*

*Reflect on a sexual desire you have and see what voices come up to warn you or keep you safe. If you are looking to provoke yourself, google a type of porn you are interested in but think of as naughty and possibly inappropriate. Perhaps it's even the thought of watching porn, period, that brings up your critic.*

See what voices come up saying something like, "I could never do that because...." Write down what comes up.

Get to know these voices, listen to them; they are a part of you. It's all good; let them know they are heard and that you will move forward with those thoughts in mind.

# RELEASE

Once you know what critical voices are coming up, you are able to do something constructive with them. If you have any reservations about continuing on your path of desire after doing your review above, read on!

This stage is the most fascinating for me because it's the point where action has been done. I've lived something out. I've reflected on it, and now I get to decide if this experience will be the end of the road for this desire or if it's the start of expanding on it. It's a powerful intersection.

After my experience with John, I knew what it felt like to follow through; I knew what it brought up for me, and now it was time to decide how I was going to evolve my desire and self as a result.

## INTEGRATION

I want to introduce another paradox here. Release, I mean true release involves integration, not rejection or elimination. Letting go doesn't come from pushing away the parts of ourselves that are dark, but by letting them be a part of our life and seeing their value.

Following sexual desires involves bringing up judgments about ourselves and figuring out how to work with them when they surface.

When I had sex with John, one of the things that came to mind was, "I'm a slut." The initial thought of it was, "Ugh, I don't want to be a slut. That sounds bad." Shortly after those thoughts surfaced, I was having a conversation with someone about my resistance to being a slut and they suggested I ask David to call me a slut in the bedroom and see what happens.

Well, I went home and I asked him to do it, and as we were having sex that week he said in a raw and primal way, "Are you my dirty little slut?" As he leaned over me from behind with one hand on my hip and the other around my neck, the word *"yes"* flowed out of me effortlessly as my body sunk into a blissful state.

It was more than a relief to admit it felt *good*.

Perhaps you've heard of a text called, *A Course in Miracles*? In the book, they define a miracle as a correction in perception. It may seem simple and trivial to think that a shift in perception can mean such incredible things, but our perceptions are often linked to our identity. When we create a shift in our identity, although destabilizing, it allows for a more evolved and expansive version of ourselves to come alive.

I thought, "Wow... I like being called a slut, I like the idea of being a slut in some contexts." Super interesting, to say the least. Mind blown in a fabulous way.

When I realized there was a context in which I enjoyed thinking of myself as a slut. the word lost its negative charge for me. I've seen time and time again that when I integrate what I've judged, the emotional charge is released.

What trips me up is when I'm so emotionally thrown off or charged from a thought that I can't see the possibilities past the block. I'm either taking it too seriously, only seeing the downside to it, or thinking that my association to it has to mean "bad things" to or for me.

The way I feel release from the negatively charged emotion is to integrate what I have resisted and to feel into the emotional charge so that it can become part of what fuels me.

LET IT IN TO LET IT GO

When I went through a rough patch after my experimentation with non-monogamy, I had what felt like an identity crisis. I was trying to re-figure out who I was and what I would need in order to move forward.

I felt a pretty intense fear around what this all meant for me. I wanted to push away and plow through anything that felt negative from the experience.

One of the biggest challenges I shared about, when it

comes to letting desire in, is being willing to release and make peace with the parts of me that I want to control. I do this by noticing the ways it both helps and hinders me to want control and how seeking control has played a role in my life through the years.

It serves me more to acknowledge that I want to control rather than denying it or pretending I don't.

RELEASE RITUAL

A simple and powerful way to practice a release is to have a conversation with a part of yourself you are struggling with on paper. For example, if I am talking to the part of myself that feels like I need to be in control, I would ask:

- Where did you come from?
- What would you like me to know?
- What are you afraid of if I continue to follow my desire?
- What do you need more of to feel safe so we can let more in?
- How can we come together to allow me to let in more pleasure?

Keep in mind the following words by A. A. Milne, creator of Winnie the Pooh, as you sit down to write this letter: "Promise me you'll always remember: You're braver than you believe, and stronger than you seem, and smarter than you think."

You know these answers; your intuition knows them. Trust that. You are smarter than you think. You know your truth and what *you* need more than you think.

When I did this for myself, I realized the part of me that wanted control wanted me to be safe. I was reminded that making sure I have the element of safety handled to the best of my ability makes a huge difference and lowers my vigilance. It also helped me remember that baby steps are great because they allow me to keep reassessing and checking in with this fearful part of myself.

SPARK

*Set a timer for 10–15 minutes and have a conversation with a part of yourself that came up in your review. Perhaps a part of you is scared of being a bad girl, afraid of being out of control, or thinks you should feel guilty or be punished for letting in more sexual desire.*

*If it feels like it has an emotional charge, have a conversation with that part of yourself as you answer the following questions:*

- *Where did you come from?*
- *What would you like me to know?*
- *What are you afraid of if I continue to follow my desire?*
- *What do you need more of right now to feel safe so we can let more in?*
- *How can we come together to allow me to let in more pleasure?*

*It's important to know that each painful thought has an intention of keeping us safe because, as exciting as change can be, it is foreign.*

*Once you finish, read your conversation out loud. Jot down any "aha" notes of things you want to remember and then either tear up or burn your letter followed by reading the following words out loud:*

*"Universe, I surrender (insert fear and/or critical voice) to you so that I might see more clearly and know what the next best step is for me to be aligned with my highest and greatest good. I release any painful thoughts and beliefs connected to this experience and joyfully invite desire into my life. I allow myself to see how these thoughts and experiences serve me."*

*\*\*You can replace "Universe" with whatever you believe in that is Greater than you.. It can be God, Source, Your Highest Self, etc. It's all good. The thing here is to acknowledge and release.\*\**

When we share our experiences and have someone listen with an open, non-judgmental ear, we have the opportunity to be seen and release what we have been storing inside.

Sharing an experience we have been holding inside with a trusted friend is a powerful thing, especially when they are listening fully and not trying to give advice or change anything.

We all want to be seen. And this isn't about being a victim; it's about letting a part of your story be heard so that you aren't carrying the weight.

It took me a while to really get this, but there is a big difference between waking up every day complaining that you are exhausted and everything sucks and having a challenging experience that you need to process with a friend or trusted confidant.

My greatest advice, if you use this practice as a release, is the following: Tell the person you are sharing with ahead of time, "I would like to share something I experienced. I would like to share my experience and have you listen and acknowledge that you heard me. If you have any advice, maybe we can talk about that later or another time; for now, I'd just love to feel heard. When I'm done, I would love it if you said, 'Thank you for sharing.'"

## SPARK

*Try this practice above. What is something that you've been holding on to? What is a desire you have followed through on that you have a charge about (either feeling excited or challenged by it)? Call a friend and feel free to use the language above. Ask them to hold space for you as you share.*

*Remember, it's not about being a victim or having someone feel sorry for you—it's about letting all the parts of you be seen and honored.*

I learned these magic words, "Thank you for sharing," in a course I participated in, and they have been life-changing words. I like to tell people to use them with me when I don't want their advice (my significant other and I use this a lot, and it's super helpful) and to use them with other people when it feels right or when I'm at a loss for what to say.

A powerful way to release emotional charge is through something I have more than alluded to in multiple sections of this book and that is to find the activities and practices that shift your attention out of your mind into your body so you can fully feel any emotional charge you are carrying.

When I need to release an emotional charge, I dance, I OM, I masturbate, I have sex, I meditate, and feel the sensations in my body as deeply and fully as possible.

Emotions can get intense and it's a practice to feel them, but the path of sexual pleasure requires more feeling. I haven't found a way to experience more pleasure without having to experience more pain. I don't mean this negatively. I just mean that you can't select what you want to feel more of if you want to feel more pleasure. If you choose to start feeling more, you *do* feel more...of everything.

It's a practice. To release the emotional charge from an experience, learn to feel more.

I will repeat: *It's a practice.* It will feel challenging initially because, in general, in today's society, we aren't raised to feel, be in our bodies, and tune in to sensations. We are taught to think, and do, and get it done.

Stay with the sensations you feel as long as you can when they come up and find activities that help you drop into your body.

This is a reason I love masturbation and I recommend

doing it without any porn or stimulus besides your finger and some lube. Draw all your attention to the sensations you are feeling in your body, stay with them as long as you can and see if you can amplify them with your attention. Dancing is another way I do this; when I move, I drop my attention into my muscles and can move to music that fits how I feel without dwelling on the emotion.

# SPARK

*Start a practice that involves the deliberate intention of learning to feel more.*

*Here are a few practices where you can try this.*


TOUCH YOURSELF:

*Lay down on your bed with some lube to your side. Turn off technology, except maybe to set a timer if that feels good. Don't have any stimulus coming in to direct your attention anywhere outside of your body.*

*Perhaps you put a towel underneath you, and either half naked or fully naked (your preference) begin to touch yourself. Sometimes I like to start at my clitoris, this nerve-packed, high-sensation powerhouse of a body part. Sometimes I like to start at my feet. Let your hands lead.*

*The idea here is bring all of your attention to body sensation and feeling. When you notice sensation rising, stay with it. Feel it as intensely as possible. See what happens as you let it intensify.*

*Notice how it feels to be sexual without the goal of a finish line except to feel.*

BODY SCANS:

If this concept of feeling is new and feels a bit scary, a great place to start is with a guided body scan, and this can be easily searched on youtube.com. Search "body scan" in the search tool and find one with a voice that feels soothing. Find a quiet spot where you can lay down and do the scan. Find one that takes you through different parts of your body from head to toe while you notice the sensations in each part of your body as you move through the exercise.

# PART IV
# WHAT I KNOW OF
# PLEASURE

# THE GAME

When I experience pleasure, I want to have more pleasure. This might sound like a no-brainer, but sometimes I can be a slow learner. When I experience more pleasure, I want to do more, be more, give more, and engage more.

I write this because I have caught myself thinking that pleasure is not a great thing for productivity, that it's distracting and something to fear.

I no longer feel this way.

Genuine pleasure is always a life-giving and energizing thing. When I sat down to write this book, I looked back and wrote about the times in my life when I forgot pleasure and I went too far into a mode of work or resisting pleasure. I lost my aliveness and everything felt exhausting. When I allow pleasure, something in me is like, "Alright, let's do this."

I can't tell you how many times I have said, "I don't want to have sex," or "Don't touch me," only to find out that when my partner gave me a gentle nudge and kissed me, or made a move to have sex, I *did* want it. Sometimes when I get moody, David will say to me, "You need some lovin' baby, don't you." And I'll say, "No," with my mouth, but my eyes and my inviting smile will say, "Yes, please." It's become our playful game at this point.

I'm starting to see the moments more and more where my head is not being true to the voice of my body and desire. This knowledge has taught me to slow down and ask myself if my response is reactive and knee-jerk or if it's authentic to what I really want.

More sex in my life translates into more energy. When writing this book, sometimes when I needed to regroup or was getting too much into my head, I would stop for a dance break or a masturbation break to get out of my head and into my body. In my body is where the alchemy happens. It's where the life comes from and all the foggy stuff and the stagnant energy gets recycled into fuel.

There were times in my life that if you told me, "To have a life with pleasure, you have to experience pleasure in the first place," I wouldn't have believed you. I might have even scoffed at you.

Now I know it to be true. Pleasure is sparked and fueled by experiences that bring pleasure.

One of the things I thought was that I had to earn it first, or someone had to earn it. But then no one, including myself, was ever good enough to earn it when I got stuck in that thought pattern.

It became a bit of a game. I'll let myself experience pleasure *when...*

I would use this one to withhold sex. When I was upset in relationships, I purposely denied sex. I would get angry that my man didn't do the errands I asked him to, or I'd feel hurt by something he said, and instead of accepting a sexual advance, I would reject it. I'd be like, "Hahaha," with a malicious laugh in my head, thinking I stuck it to him. But wait, was that really what was happening?

The only thing either of us was being stuck with was a bad mood. We were frustrated and disconnected from one another. Withholding sex does not lead to resolution. Connection, playfulness, and empathy have a far better chance, and sexy time is quite often something that can get those juices flowing.

# SPARK

To get to know yourself better and your resistance to pleasure, on a blank piece of paper write down the sentence starter, "I'll give myself pleasure when..." As you've done throughout the book, set a timer for five minutes and continue to finish this sentence starter.

Once you have seen what comes up there, set another five-minute timer and change your sentence starter to, "I want to give myself pleasure when...."

Look back and see what came up as you finished these sentence starters. Do you cut yourself off from pleasure more than you realize? Which list makes you feel more energized and alive?

Are you ready to make pleasure practices a greater part of your day-to-day life?

## REMEMBER THE CHOICE

L ife without pleasure and connection to my desire feels like I am living in a cold, frigid place, which is very tiring. When I go a few weeks without sex, masturbation, playful flirtation, or infusing my day with something that makes me feel sexy, I'll start to push sex away. I won't have as much fun with my life, and I'll take everything *way* too seriously.

Heck, I'm in a moment where if I don't have sex of some kind every few days, I'll start to feel the effects of coldness seeping in. I'll scold the slap to the ass, and I'll push away the embrace. When I catch it, I'll know I've gone too long without touch or physical pleasure.

I have to consciously notice how long I have gone without play and choose to play again.

I try to surround myself and reach out to people who will remind me to take myself less seriously. If I am too serious for too long, I'll know I have to get back to pleasure.

# SPARK

*As you reflect while reading this book, ask yourself how often you let your day be infused with pleasure, sex, and desire? And what happens when you put pleasure on the back burner?*

*How often do you let yourself have a moment to put the lip gloss on that feels and smells delicious, wear the panties that make you feel sexy, or smile at the cashier where you get your morning coffee and have a playful interaction?*

*Do you ask for the sex you want? Do you have as much sex as you'd like? How often do you touch yourself or give yourself the gift of someone else's touch?*

*Reflect on these questions and practice giving yourself the permission to do more activities that bring you pleasure as an experiment. I dare you to prove me wrong. Prove to me that more self-loving pleasure doesn't lead to more productivity in the long run. Bet you can't!*

# CONCLUSION

Desire tends to ask something of me I have never given. Desire asks me to evolve. It asks me to be new every day and to find a way to identify my roadblocks, my doubts, all the places I lock myself down so that I can really and truly see them. It wants me to pay attention and not always in a pretty way.

I'll wake up one day and want to make out with one of my girlfriends, and I won't be able to forget about it, or I'll want to resolve a conflict I've had for two years and have been fighting with sticking my head in the sand about. I'll know without a doubt that I have to publish the book that has been in my heart for three years. I'll want to ask my man if he can fuck me in a way he hasn't done before.

Desire can be truly relentless in the most excruciating and fabulous ways. It is not logical or linear, and it can feel scattered and messy. I love to compare my relationship with desire to my relationship with sex because there are so many overlaps. They can both feel awkward and involve getting naked in one way or another, but they can be a lot of fun and a true adventure full of sensation.

This is your juicy and enticing entry point. Once you start to hear the whispers and let the voice of your desire get louder, in my experience, that baby gets a voice of its own: Your True Voice, and it can't be turned off.

Pleasure will come as a result of listening to your desire. The pleasure might not be immediate or in the way you'd expect, but it will come. To get the most of it, it will require you to feel and get to know what you have labeled as good and bad within yourself. If you are anything like me, you will want things that you thought were bad and you will question what it means to be good.

Listening to your desires will equip you with the inner strength to keep going through the hard days. The momentum becomes so strong that you don't have to work for it as much anymore. Commit to your desire, especially your sexual desire. It will be loyal to you. Loyalty to your desire is the ultimate and most rewarding commitment one can make.

You are worth it. You desire wants you, and I bet you want it too if you've made it through.

If this book helps you wake up your desire even a little bit, you can bet I'm doing a happy dance for you.

# RESOURCES

*For more information about Jaclyn, to get email updates, and for information on upcoming books, go to:*
*jaclynlaceyfoster.com*

## Schools:

SFactor

www.sfactor.com

One Taste

https://onetaste.us/

## Books:

The Multi-Orgasmic Woman

*Mantak Chia & Rachel Carlton Abrams, M.D.*

Slow Sex: The Art and Craft of the Female Orgasm

*Nicole Daedone*

The Breakthrough Experience: A Revolutionary New Approach to Personal Transformation

*Dr. John F. Demartini*

# ACKNOWLEDGMENTS

I would like to thank every person on my path that encouraged me to follow through when this book was just an idea that I could barely fathom bringing to life. To Jeremy who received a page a day of babble as I was creating momentum and new habits to bring this book to life.

To all my Priscilla's buddies that asked me how it was going and kept my dream fresh in my mind. To Self-Publishing School for giving me structure and the final push to put a deadline to my dream as well as the baby steps to make it all feel so doable.

To Hannah, my editor for encouraging me to be willing to be detailed in my story, helping me to drill down what I wanted to say, and getting me to own that my deeper desire was to go beyond talking about desire in general to talking about sexual desire.

A big massive thank you to David, my partner who has supported me through both processes of book creation and sexual liberation since the day we met. David, you supported me sharing more than just my life, but *our* life with such grace and warmth. You are the perfect person to share this journey with and I can't thank you enough for all the ways you meet me where I am at, help me grow, and make me a stronger, wiser and more turned on woman.

A big thank you as well to Liz, Diana, Jess, and Max for your input, encouragement and feedback as I was finalizing the book and bringing it all together.

# ABOUT THE AUTHOR

Jaclyn is an author, speaker, and coach. For years, she traveled and lived in different countries including New Zealand, Spain, and France on a mission to narrow down what got her most excited in this world and sexual liberation is where she has landed with enthusiasm. Though born and raised in Massachusetts, after moving back to the US, she found herself with an opportunity to live on the outskirts of Los Angeles. Since living in LA she has immersed herself in the world of pleasure, sexual exploration, and the discovery of what it takes to live a life where she is led by her desire.

She currently lives on the outskirts of Los Angeles with her partner and their adorable Jack Russell doggie, Angel. As a self-proclaimed self-help junkie, you will often find her in the middle of three books at once, to be found stacked up on her bedroom end table. Her favorite spot in the house is outside on the porch overlooking the garden so she can listen to the birds, enjoying the fresh air with a book or journal in hand.

To learn more about Jaclyn and follow her, come visit:

Website: jaclynlaceyfoster.com

 instagram.com/fosterjaclyn